# ROAM WASN'T BUILT IN A DAY

## The *Adventures* of

## GUY VAN CLEVE

1960 · VOL. I · 1975

Printed in the United States of America
First Printing, 2024
ISBN 979-8-9882428-6-4 (eBook)
ISBN 979-8-9882428-5-7 (paperback)
ISBN 978-1-946292-51-3 (hardcover)

*For my friend, Natchez Morice, a master of living life, making friends and storytelling extraordinaire.*

TABLE OF CONTENTS

I**T'S A WILD** but wonderful experience to write a book. This one represents many, many years of work searching and finding the right ghost that could overlay her writing with my voice. I have had four ghosts before finding the *Eureka* fifth. Over the years, my friends and family have been steadfast in their encouragement to reduce my favorite party and social storytelling to a book. *Voila!* It is now finally done. I was blessed with equal helpings of Wonderlust and Wanderlust and my sitting in one place long enough to write any book, including mine, was out of the question. I always fended off my more insistent friends and family members by reminding them that my favorite high school English teacher was right when she would give me low scores on my term papers, because as she put it, "I was always dangling too many of my participles." I thereafter would rest my case and always seemed to be granted a reprieve. Nevertheless, I continued my search for a ghost that could magically convert my storytelling to ink on page and now, to my friends and readers, this is it.

First, I must thank my ex-wife, Pat, who, for the full twenty years of our marriage, hounded me (in a good way) to share my stowaway story both with new friends we met along the way and to WRITE A BOOK. She was instrumental in keeping this flame lit regardless of anything else that life threw our way.

Second, I must thank my great literary best friend and cheerleader, Joyce Bone, who has believed in the telling of my story for over a dozen years and who has painstakingly read and reviewed each ghost's work leading up to this moment of release. Her time and encouragement is equally responsible for this book's contribution to what joy may come from its reading.

And most importantly, thank you, Candi Cross of You Talk I Write, for bringing her unique and uncanny genius to this effort to make writing and sharing this book a reality.

Finally, whenever I think of my journey, I think of all those named or otherwise identified herein, who were, without question, the light in the room of my life—thank you!

# *Lush Life*

*"Life is short, break the rules, forgive quickly, kiss slowly, love truly, laugh uncontrollably and never regret anything that made you smile. Twenty years from now, you will be more disappointed by the things you didn't do than by the ones you did. So throw off the bowlines. Sail away from the safe harbor. Catch the trade winds in your sails. Explore. Dream. Discover."*

—Mark Twain

I'VE LIVED MY life in colors and textures. My existence has been governed by my senses. I see every experience on land and sea and in the air as the nectar of the gods—and I encourage people I come in contact with to embrace the same outlook. Our innate ability to see, feel, hear, smell and taste life is an extraordinary gift one in the same as breathing.

Life can be measured by the amount of pleasure we've consumed rather than the losses and heartaches we've suffered. Of course, both make us human, but let's choose more beauty, stimulation, and exhilaration . . . wherever we are! Watch the world's joy scale go up exponentially!

Just as Mark Twain delighted readers in the mid 19th century adventures with exploits of Tom Sawyer and Huckleberry Finn, so does this author wish to convey the same delights from his mid 20th century stage appearance and pursuit of adventure.

Each day is a fresh opportunity to pursue that which drives your senses. You don't have to stay transfixed in a state of wanderlust. You can wander and roam without going far or even spending money. In the following pages, I'll show you how.

# CHAPTER I

# *Forbidden Places*

*"You must go on adventures to find
out where you truly belong."*

—Sue Fitzmaurice

**EVERYONE KNEW ABOUT** the old trestle. It was The Place You Weren't Allowed to Go. Moms across the town of Lynchburg, Virginia would tell their little ones in the most stern, but Christian terms to stay the hell away from it.

"Keep clear of that place after school."

"Don't even think of going there with your friends."

"If I hear you've been on that trestle, you'll be in for a whoopin' you'll never forget."

Just about everyone in town could tell you the name of someone—once or twice removed—who was killed or had lost a leg by being dumb enough to wander down the rusty railroad tracks that ran across that bridge. If you ventured the 200 or so yards out to the middle and suddenly spotted one of those Norfolk Southern engines chugging toward you, there was no way you'd make it safely to the other side in time. You were already a goner.

Jumping off the trestle into the water below was an even surer way to die, given that it stood about fifteen stories above the James River. Hitting the scattered, rock-bedded water from that high was certain death.

Most everybody knew when, each day, a train was supposed to cross that bridge, on the outskirts of Lynchburg. The *whoooooo* of the conductor's whistle echoed through that part of town on a regular pattern, like the sun rising and setting, or the crowds leaving the courthouse exactly at noon every day for lunch. You came to anticipate it and when you didn't hear it at the proper time, you noticed its absence without even thinking.

The problem was the unexpected trains. The ones coming from, and leading to, parts unknown. They didn't pass through Lynchburg often, but still, they did appear, and they occasionally took an unsuspecting victim off that trestle. Maybe it was a drunk stumbling across its span on a shortcut to the river's opposite bank; or a teenager smoking a cigarette with a couple of friends, with their legs hanging off the side on a lazy, summer afternoon; or maybe even just a kid, running across it on a dare.

When I was in high school, a good friend of mine, Buddy Miller, walked out to the middle with a couple of friends when one of those unexpected trains came. He had nowhere to go. One of the guys was close enough to the riverbank to run to safety. Another was seriously hurt. Buddy was hit and thrown into the river. It was one of the saddest days of my life.

Yet despite the obvious dangers presented by this towering collection of tarnished steel girders built before World

War I, I saw it in a different light than the mothers of Lynchburg. To me, the trestle represented freedom, a gateway to different worlds. As a young kid, I watched the trains leaving town across it with jealousy, like the guy in the Johnny Cash song, "Folsom Prison Blues." I wanted to go escape the bars of my life and follow them to exotic locales like Roanoke, Charlottesville, Harrisonburg and beyond.

Walking along the tall banks of the railroad tracks, I fantasized about jumping from the tall, grassy banks above the trestle and landing atop one of the cars, clinging on top with a death grip as it crossed the river and disappeared into the foothills. Finally, I said to myself, "Why not just do it?" Like every other red-blooded American male, I was born with an X and Y chromosome, but as my life unfurled, I came to learn my Y chromosome really turned out to be a *Y not* chromosome.

No more fantasizing. It was time to take action! I was darned if I wasn't going to jump off one of those banks and onto a train. After all, I was old enough to take care of myself. I'd blown enough candles off my birthday cakes, for cryin' out loud!

The day of action finally arrived and I climbed into position. I heard the train's loud whistle sounding before the engine appeared. It was the sound of freedom calling! I readied myself on the bank, about twenty feet above the tracks, right at the edge of the trestle. If I somehow stumbled and missed my mark, even the best-case scenario was pretty bad. If I didn't fall off the car and get run over, I stood the very good chance of bouncing down the steep embankment to the river – not that these prospects ever occurred to me in the slightest.

The train's engine approached, and slowed as it crossed

the trestle, the structure's ancient steel frame groaning beneath its weight. I spotted my target: the roof of a car a short way down the line. I timed the jump in my head. *Twenty seconds . . . Fifteen . . . Ten . . . Five, four, three, two, one . . . go!*

I leaped from my position and into the air, carried by faith, foolhardiness, and excitement for the unknown. I would come to feel this exact same thrill a little later in life, as I jumped aboard the world's largest cruise ship from a terminal pier in Hawaii, with no ticket, money, or passport, on my journey around the world.

CHAPTER II

# *On the Edge of Nature*

*"To awaken quite alone in a strange town is
one of the pleasantest sensations in the world.
You are surrounded by adventure."*

—Freya Stark

**MISERY. FORCED RELOCATION.** The world as I knew it was
over. Those were the thoughts racing through my head
during my family's move to Lynchburg, Virginia. I had
spent the first seven years of my life in Richmond, after all.
It was all I knew.

My dad, Chuck, was an insurance man. When he
returned from fighting in World War II, he graduated from
college, and like so many former GIs in the booming 1950s,
found himself with a wealth of job options with large corporate employers. He took a position in Richmond working
for the Hartford Insurance Company.

From my recollection, my family's life in the capital
of Virginia was a comfortable one. If you've never been to
Richmond, it's a surprisingly cosmopolitan city, kind of a

light, smaller-scale version of Atlanta. It is among America's oldest major cities placed on the map with Patrick Henry, a U.S. Founding Father, who famously declared, "Give me liberty or give me death" at its St. John's Church in 1775, leading to the Revolutionary War. Even at a very young age, I loved the access to history, culture and, most importantly, friends.

All of my near-aged buddies lived within a few densely populated blocks, meaning fun and entertainment were always a short walk away. We played football and baseball in the neighborhood parks at will and enjoyed pool parties throughout the spring, summer, and early fall.

If one group of friends was busy or not around, I'd find the group a block away or another group in a different direction. The options were endless. It felt like Disneyland before Disney had invented it. In fact, my nickname from the time I was able to walk out the front door without hand-held assistance was "Where's Guy?" because my parents were never quite sure where I was and were always wondering, *where is that boy?*

Best of all, inside my Richmond life was that my parents raised me as an only child. If you need verification, just ask my sister. She was born more than a decade after I was, and by the time she could speak, I had practically already left home. You'll hear more about my flying the coop later though.

Everything changed for me in 1960. If you're a history buff, you might think of that year as the one when the Soviets shot down a U.S. spy plane flown by Gary Powers, or when John F. Kennedy was elected President. To me though, something even more world-changing happened: we left Richmond.

In a seven-year-old city boy's mind, Lynchburg was about one hundred miles due west of absolutely nowhere, at the foot of the Blue Ridge Mountains, which looked like towering fortress walls. My dad's new job with a different insurance company gave him a prestigious territory of the entire State of Virginia. His bosses figured that if he was based in Lynchburg, given its central location, he could access all the company's offices and agencies more easily, and with significantly less driving. I could have given them 1,001 reasons why their reasoning was completely dumb, but let the record show that no one ever asked the seven-year-old.

So, it was off to Lynchburg, an old tobacco and railroad town—and for the last four days of the Civil War, the capital of Virginia—on the broad, slow-rolling James River. On the ride to our new home in the family sedan, I considered how the best days of my life had already ended forever. In Richmond, I had tons of friends; I liked my school and I liked my house. Both sets of grandparents lived there, and I saw them often. I even had a steady, seven-year-old girlfriend who was smitten with glee every time we were together. Now, all that was fading out of sight in the rear-view mirror.

I kept asking myself: *What did I do wrong? Am I being punished?*

I understood the back-story, but damn, it just didn't seem fair. So, I stowed a plan in the back of my mind to somehow find a way to return to my one-and-only hometown and maybe live with one set of my grandparents—it didn't matter which. I thought, *Y'all go to Lynchburg, Mom and Dad. But I'm going back to Richmond (somehow). I'll keep in touch!*

This idea hardened like a pile of wet cement during my

first few weeks in Lynchburg. Talk about culture shock! It was more like cultural electrocution. In Richmond, there were five movie theaters. Out my door were a million adventures, waiting for me. I used to walk to Willow Lawn Shopping Center and down Monument Avenue just to marvel at the traffic, people, and commotion.

In Lynchburg, there was only one movie theater. When I stepped out the front door of our modest two-story house, all I saw were boring, old oak trees and broad lawns separating quiet houses. There were no people milling about the sidewalk, and there was no commotion—unless you count the squirrels getting in a territorial fight.

Directly next-door was a massive, thousand-acre, Presbyterian orphanage that also doubled as a self-sustaining farm, worked by the children who lived there. A city mouse had arrived in the country and very much wanted to turn around.

We had moved in the middle of summer vacation, and since I had no friends in Lynchburg, I spent most of my initial days wandering through the vast tracts of nearby woodlands that rose into the forested foothills, trying to get lost. As I went, I surveyed my surroundings fearlessly like I was Daniel Boone or Davy Crockett. Richmond did have some small woodsy areas, but they were enclosed within parks. This was very different. My explorations took me everywhere. No cave was too small or too snake infested for me to crawl into. No body of water too broad to cross. No boundaries or limitations. I was born without the fear gene; in its place was a deep sense of curiosity and adventure that continues to guide me through life to this very day. Though I didn't want to admit it at the time, living on the edge of nature was the perfect situation for an explorer like me.

I wouldn't say that I warmed up to Lynchburg as the months dragged on, but I thawed like an iceberg, melting slowly. I still harbored the idea of running off to live with my grandparents, but I also began making friends and including them in my adventures. We used the woods as our playground, building tree houses and forts, holding club meetings in caves. I was usually the instigator.

Every morning, I thought, *what lands can I conquer?* There's a sense of restlessness in my life that has sent me endlessly chasing after adventure, like Captain Ahab seeking the great, white whale in Melville's *Moby Dick*. This mindset has guided me daily throughout my travels and life. You're probably wondering how my parents allowed me to disappear for hour after hour. For the most part, they didn't have a choice. Even if they forbade me from leaving the house, I was too restless to keep indoors. Literally, I couldn't help but escape! If there was one subject they could agree upon as husband and wife, it was being frustrated with me for disappearing. I was constantly living up to my "Where's Guy?" moniker.

# CHAPTER III

# Lucidity in the Caves

*"I went to the woods because I wished to live deliberately,
to front only the essential facts of life, and see if I
could not learn what it had to teach, and not, when
I came to die, discover that I had not lived."*

—Henry David Thoreau

**MY PARENTS MET** as college students and came from two very different backgrounds. My father was fresh from serving in World War II, and, as you can imagine, his experiences in the European Theater left a deep impression upon him. His job during the war was to shimmy up trees and makeshift telephone poles to hang communication wires so that American army units spread across the area could talk to each other. He didn't tell me much about his experiences, but he did explain once how nearly every night in camp, there would be one less of his guys in the unit hanging and running the communication wires, having fallen victim to enemy gunfire.

They weren't behind enemy lines, but they were mostly in advanced positions and vulnerable to snipers. When they returned from their work at the end of the day, my dad and the other men with him would open a bottle of whiskey and say, "Shit, we lived another day." He would maintain that talent for enjoying a stiff drink, or five, for the rest of his shortened life.

After the war ended and he arrived back home to the States, his mother wouldn't let him keep idle for long. For her, a lazy person wasn't worth the powder it took to blow them to Hades. Within a week of my dad's return home, she told him, "Okay, you start at the University of Richmond on Monday."

"Damned if I do," he said.

"Damned if you don't," she said back.

There he was, a 6'2", blond-haired, blue-eyed, string bean of a war hero who had just helped beat the Germans and survived to tell the story. He wanted to relax for a while and raise hell like a normal twenty-something-year-old, but my grandmother wasn't having any of that. He dug in his feet and repeated that he wasn't going to school.

"It's not up for discussion. You're going to college. If you don't, I'm going to get your daddy to give you a differ-ent education!"

My grandfather was a Richmond police sergeant and had a strong manner of will and authority that my father feared even more than he did the Germans, so off to uni-versity he went.

He started at the University of Richmond the next Monday. While there, he joined a fraternity of mostly World War II veterans and hard drinkers. They used to drive up to Fredericksburg on weekends to mix with the students at Mary Washington College, an all-women's school at the time, where my mother was attending classes. She was a teetotaler who came from a family of Temperance Union-belonging, god-fearing, tambourine-shaking Christians.

My mother and father met at one of those old-fashioned Southern college mixers one weekend afternoon, and somehow the subject of tennis came up. She was quite good at the sport, and for him, the topic was a good a way to break the ice. He invited her out to play tennis, completely underestimating her abilities. When they met for the match, she whipped him up and down the court and really tanned his hide.

Afterward, my father got back to his fraternity and said, "By God, ain't no Yankee woman gonna whoop a good ole Southern boy. I'll be damned if I don't right this wrong!"

For the next two weeks he and his buddies played tennis constantly. He invited her out for a match a second time and won. From there, it was L-O-V-E.

Even after they married, their passion for the sport never faltered. When I was growing up, I watched them play tennis all the time and began hitting tennis balls with them. By seven or eight years old, I was taking lessons, and by age ten, I was able to serve and return the ball quite well. My parents' tennis obsession also became mine. The sport introduced me to my first, true love in high school, and I still play on several leagues today.

Tennis has also taught me many valuable life lessons such as solving problems while staying nimble on my feet, and using critical thinking to approach challenges, hard shots and roadblocks. It also taught me to maintain alertness and to focus on the task at-hand while identifying the strengths and weaknesses of my opponents. Most importantly, it taught me humility. Tennis can be a very humbling sport, for there is always a faster gun in the West.

One of my idols is the former tennis great, Arthur Ashe,

who once said, "Success is a journey, not a destination. The doing is often more important than the outcome." This quote exemplifies how I've spent my life; I've always concerned myself with the journey, the doing, without much regard for the destination or outcome. I saw my mentor, Ashe, as doing the same. He won three Grand Slam tennis singles titles and was the first black player selected to the United States Davis Cup team. He was also the only black man to ever win the singles title at Wimbledon, the US Open *and* the Australian Open.

I actually met Arthur Ashe in Richmond when I was 10 years old. Richmond used to host tennis clinics at the elementary schools in the summer and he showed up to one of them. He would bounce from school to school to appear at them sometimes, spending ten or fifteen minutes with each kid in a summer tennis camp program; he was a marvelously giving person like that.

I happened to be at one of these clinics during a visit from Lynchburg to see my grandparents. I took every opportunity to get back to Richmond as often as I could. Ashe spent a snippet of time helping me work on my game, and the way he connected with me felt like we'd caught lightning in a bottle. That's what I'd call it: *lightning in a bottle.* That moment became the highlight of my life. From that point on, I was obsessed with experiencing more of these highlights.

Back in Lynchburg, I was making more friends, but as I grew older, I was happiest when I explored by myself, without any concern for the time of day. When I was exploring with friends, they were ever mindful of logistical concerns, and because I was not, exploring alone soon became the only way to go.

I began to learn the names of the plants around me and quietly came to observe birds and animals before they scattered out of sight. My mother gave me copies of *Adventures of Huckleberry Finn* and *The Adventures of Tom Sawyer* and the characters and scenes came to life for me in those woods near my house. I carried a pair of wire cutters with me wherever I went for any barbed wire fence that might have occasionally blocked my direction of travel.

I especially loved those Virginia mountain caves. The state as a whole contains some 4,000 caves, and the local legend was that Confederate gold was still hidden in some of them. Whenever I walked over hill and dale, or moved a tree branch to spot a cave, I'd climb in it like it was mine. Other kids who tried would occasionally get bitten by snakes, like a rattler or a copperhead, slithering in the crags. It would just about kill them, but because no one ever died, I was never dissuaded.

The caves were so dark and dank, much like being in the dungeon of a castle. Sometimes their passageways would lead me to the woods through a different entrance, and other times, they dead-ended. Some were spacious enough to walk through on foot, and others I'd need to belly-crawl through, squeezing my pint-sized body among the cracks that were often lit by barely more than a suggestion of sunlight or my flashlight.

It was in these caves that the true wonder of discovering new places and experiences awakened within me like a hungry bear coming out of hibernation. I began craving more adventures, newer wonders, and looked for them wherever – and whenever – I could manage to escape my school or home.

# CHAPTER IV

# Train Hopping to the Old Frontier

*"Life should not be a journey to the grave with the intention of arriving safely in a pretty and well-preserved body, but rather to skid in broadside in a cloud of smoke, thoroughly used up, totally worn out, and loudly proclaiming 'Wow! What a Ride!'"*

—Hunter S. Thompson

**BEFORE MY FIRST** jump at the trestle, I scouted the scene for a while, figuring out where and how to do it. The trains leaving town followed a set of winding tracks carved into the mountainside, and the engines always slowed down as it approached the trestle. I noticed that if I climbed the grassy banks that rose just before the edge of the trestle, I could drop onto the top of a moving boxcar safely and with almost no effort. "It's as easy as sliding down a greased pole backwards," I would tell myself.

Or, at least, "easy" in a kid's mind, without any regard

for the dangers of the jump. After all, I didn't need to swing onto it with a rope, like Tarzan with his vine, nor did I need to run to catch up to it in order to climb aboard. With every passing day, my motivation to hop on one of those trains and ride it somewhere – anywhere – grew stronger. As far as I was concerned, there were places to go and people to see. Finally, on one glorious summer morning, I mustered up the nerve to do it. I could feel the determination in my bones. Sweat collected in my palms as I thought of the sweet success to come. To me, succeeding meant tripling the possibility of adventures I could have on any one given day.

In one super heroic leap, my agile body became one with the moving boxcar. I was pure motion and exhilaration.

When the train sped up, I turned onto my stomach for better balance, and when it slowed down, I'd sit cross-legged or leaned on my elbow, watching an amazing new world fly by me on either side. On that first train ride, I realized that I wasn't like the Folsom Prison convict in that Johnny Cash song after all, for the cell door in front of me, the one holding me back from adventure, was never locked in the first place; I just needed the courage and initiative to walk up and push it open. From that moment forward, I vowed that I would never allow myself to be stuck in the prison of an ordinary life. *I'd be a free agent instead.*

The scenery on that first trip kept me wide-eyed the whole time as the Blue Ridge Mountains rose around me in every direction, the landscape adorned with white pine, hemlock, oak, maple and rhododendron as far as the eye could see. I passed tumbling slopes of glassy, trout-filled rivers and streams that were so crisp and clear, it would make your mouth water and tiny station houses that were carved into the narrow mountain hollows. Unbeknownst to me, I really *was* beginning to love the wilderness of the woods near my home.

When the train stopped in Bedford, a farming and factory town about 40 miles from Lynchburg, I climbed off at the old, stonewalled train station and began my exploration. Walking through downtown Bedford is like stepping through a time machine; the streets were lined with old, two-story shops and storefronts that were built in the horse-and-buggy days. Standing in the middle of the town, a classic Greek Revival-style courthouse caught my eye, and at the corner of Main Street and North Bridge stood an ancient yet charming 15-foot-tall clock that would gently notify passersby of the time.

After a few hours of wandering, watching and meeting new people, I decided to hitchhike home. I wasn't along the side of the road for long before someone, a traveling salesman driving a sedan, pulled over.

"Where you going, young boy?" he said through his rolled-down window.

"I'm going to Lynchburg, Virginia," I replied.

"I can get you part of the way, but not all the way."

"Well, just get me as far as you can get me," I said all too confidently, trying to act a few years older, and much more sophisticated, than I actually was.

Within a couple of hours, I was home—my parents none the wiser. As far as they knew, I had just been wandering around the woods as usual.

Success! Whenever I got the chance over the next couple of years, I stowed away on a boxcar and rode west, always west. To me, that was the direction of the old frontier—encompassing mystery, survival, adventure, and intrigue. I went to Bedford a lot and as I grew more experienced and courageous, my trips extended to Charlottesville, Roanoke, and faraway specks on the map whose names I don't even remember anymore. I let fate take me where it wanted to on those trains. Some would go left at a fork and head south; some would turn north. It didn't matter to me.

To get home from those expeditions, I always hitch-hiked. The car rides were often the most memorable part of the whole trip. Even more than I loved telling stories of adventures, I loved hearing such stories from the new faces I'd meet. The back-and-forth chatter during those car rides was captivating—like the best movies and TV shows all rolled into one. They usually started with me piping up and asking the driver something simple like, "Hey, what do you do?"

From there, the conversation usually took off like a bottle rocket on the Fourth of July. I met farmers, house-wives, students, traveling salesmen and tradesmen. I would innocently ask questions about where they were from and what they did, if they liked their lot in life, and they always gladly and willingly shared their stories with me.

These folks gave me such an amazing new perspective on human culture and what it meant to be an adult. As I'd listen to their tales of victories, tragedies, hard knocks and windfalls, they'd enlighten me about experiences and endeavors I had never even heard of before. In doing so, they showcased the beauty and joy that could always be found, even in the most mundane of lives. Then, there were the jokes! For example, if I were to get into a car with a salesman, I knew that I would be belly-laughing all the way to my next stop, wherever that destination may be.

I learned so much more about life and the human condition from hitchhiking than I ever could have by, say, sitting in a classroom with someone pointing a ruler at me to keep my book open—that was the reason why I so often opted for the less formal education I gained from train-hopping versus spending days in school. Through these trips, I became enamored with relating to the human experience, and I still haven't let go of that passion to this day.

Usually, the hitchhiking trip home took about twice as long as the train did to get me somewhere. I used that measurement to estimate my turnaround time. So, if I rode the tracks, say, for four hours, I knew I'd need at least eight hours to make the return trip home. Sometimes I would blow the estimates out the door and get home late at night. The best thing then was to just climb through my bedroom window as quietly as I could so my parents couldn't hear my return.

They didn't like for me to miss dinner, but when I did, they normally assumed that I was just at a friend's house eating with their family. I was a frequent and welcomed guest at many of the neighborhood supper tables. Sure, they worried about me, but it was a low-grade worry rather than a full-on panic, even if they were unsure of my exact whereabouts when retiring to bed. I spent many nights with my plethora of neighborhood friends, so, naturally, this became their default assumption. *Damn, if Guy didn't forget to call again!* they'd think to themselves. I've always subscribed to the notion that sometimes it *is* better to ask for forgiveness rather than permission, especially when permission was most likely out of the question.

After all, this was an era when kids regularly wandered around the neighborhood without showing up for dinner because they'd often be at a friend's house instead, thus, no one gave it much thought. Whenever my parents looked out the front window of our house in the evenings, no more than a minute or two would pass by before they'd see a pack of kids running in and out each other's homes or skateboarding down the street. They always assumed that I was probably mixed in with one, more, or all these groups. I was confidently resourceful, and my parents knew that I was like a cat with nine lives, I was never in any real trouble and always found my way home.

During the early morning hours when they'd wake, my parents would always peek into my room, ever so slightly opening the door, to ensure that I was home safely. I'd crack one eye open while pretending to still be asleep in order to avoid getting in too much trouble. From there, I'd walk downstairs towards breakfast, and the interrogation would begin.

"Where have you been?" one of them would ask.

"I was playing", I usually responded.

"Where?" they demanded.

"In the neighborhood."

"With who?"

"Friends," I'd declare, naming a dozen potential candidates to solidify my alibi.

"Well, we're just glad you're back," they'd state with sighful relief.

I never shared with my parents what I was *actually* doing. Everyone was better off with them thinking that I was roaming the neighborhood with other kids, or acting like Tom Sawyer and Huck Finn in the woods, but train hopping? Never.

# CHAPTER V

# The Good Wife and the Alligator

*"Always laugh when you can. It is cheap medicine."*

—Lord Byron

ONE TIME, TO put my father's nerves at ease, I took him to see the five or so treehouses that my buddies and I had built in the woods. Of those constructed, some were impressive enough to successfully relax him.

Furthermore, to keep my parents in the dark on my comings and goings, other precautions had to be taken, and I was constantly gauging their mood levels. Usually I would never enter my house through the front door, instead opting to enter the basement or climb through a window into my bedroom depending on the time of day. From there, I'd lift an ear to listen to the subject of my parents' discussions. If it were of a punitive nature, like, "When he gets home, he's going to get it," I'd quietly retreat to bed and pretend to snore if my door were to be opened. Sometimes, it worked!

Even if I caught hell, my parents usually simmered down after a good night's sleep and the repetitive yet necessary agreeance from me that they were right. After all, I never came home bruised, injured, dirty or intoxicated, and I'm sure they noted this despite my vulnerable age.

Ultimately, my parents resigned themselves to the fact that I was born with "wanderlust," and over time, they calmed down. They didn't want to constantly fight an uphill battle they knew they'd never win. The road was mostly smooth with us from there on out, especially between my dad and I, but sometimes his temper would get the best of him. This led to some tense moments, but it also led to some famously funny ones as well, like the incident of the alligator in the bathtub.

It was Christmas time the year before I moved from Richmond. My mom was a teacher at a high school in the city, not too far from our two-story home on Patterson Avenue. She and I were in the kitchen when she showed me a four-foot-long box with a baby alligator inside it.

"I've brought it home for Christmas vacation. It belongs at the school, but it can't stay there over the vacation because the school janitor cuts the heat off and this poor creature would freeze. Isn't this great?" she beamed.

"Yeah, that's pretty cool," I agreed.

You know how most babies are cute, no matter how ugly or menacing they may be once they're fully grown? Well, baby alligators aren't that way. Even in miniature form, they're like little bundles of evil: jagged teeth, unnervingly watchful, reptilian eyes and cruel smiles stretched across their long, sly mouths.

My mom started walking upstairs with the box and told me to follow her, which I did. Upon reaching the second floor, she headed into the bathroom and began filling up the tub with warm water.

"Alligators are cold-blooded, so we've got to keep this water warm enough for him. That's going to be your job," she said.

I smiled in astonishment. She was plucking my adventurous nerves. *But what about Dad?* I thought.

The tub was tall and enamel, so the critter, which was about as long as my mom's arm, fit very nicely inside it. As far as I could tell, the tub's surface was too slippery for him to climb out, granted he likely didn't try very hard, either. For the rest of that day, I kept walking into the bathroom to check on, talk to, and attempt to play with him – it was a new experience, and a fun one at that, subject to only get funnier.

In the evening, my father came home and I ran downstairs to greet him. After barely saying more than a "hello," he told my mother and I, with great dramatic effect, "God, what a day this has been! I'm going to go upstairs and wash up – I'll be back down."

I started to open my mouth to tell him about the surprise awaiting him, but my mom shot me a devilish look that told me, "Keep quiet!"

The two of us watched as my dad tromped slowly towards the second floor. We giggled. We heard the heavy clomp of his footsteps above us as he walked into the bathroom, and we giggled even more. A few more seconds passed before we heard the familiar sounds of the shower turning on. We laughed out loud as we realized just how unaware he was of the scaley surprise awaiting him a mere moment away. Alas, we heard the primal yell we had been waiting for; it roared throughout the house and out the windows, followed by a well-deserved string of lost-at-sea, sailor curses that Dad exclaimed upon finally meeting the bathroom intruder. By that point, my mother and I were in stiches, laughing hysterically at the success of our prank.

"Great goddamn! What the hell is goin' on!" he hollered.

Mom and I both bolted upstairs and found my father red with anger, surprise (or both) as he stood buck naked outside the tub.

"Did he bite you? Did you get hurt?" my mom asked him.

"No, but I'm going to get my gun right now to put an end to this alligator! Where in the hell did he come from? Who put him in the tub?"

There was no quick answer to his valid questions. He marched like Patton into the bedroom, threw on some slacks and queried, "Who wants alligator shoes?" He was as mad as a mule chewing on bumblebees. In a futile effort, my mother tried to calm him down, but she and I just couldn't resist laughing.

"No, there is no calming down. There is only about to be a dead gator," he insisted.

It would be a memory forever engrained in my brain.

As it turned out, the alligator *did* survive and returned, unscathed, to the high school where my mother taught following Christmas break. I'm not exactly sure what happened to it since then. For all I know, it could have lived to be the star of the movie, "Lake Placid."

In a household that was so often filled with laughter, the "alligator in the bathtub" incident remains one of the most memorable and hilarious moments of my childhood.

My parents were different in many ways considering that my father was a true Southern boy and my mother was a prim Connecticut Yankee, but they both had a great sense of humor, and I got a double dose of each in my DNA. Dad's humor was as dry as pavement on a hot July day; he'd deliver a deadpan, straight-faced line that could make an entire room burst into laughter, whereas my mom was just as affable and pleasant – but never sarcastic. She knew how to put a smile on people's faces the more old-fashioned way.

Over the years, my sense of humor has melded into a combination of both parents. I play poker and other friendly bar games all the time in Atlanta and will sometimes throw out a deadpan "Dad line" at the table just to bring out some laughter or even break a tense moment. Sometimes it's just a comment, other times, I'm intentionally cracking a light-hearted joke or sharing a funny observation. If it gets everyone laughing, I'm happy—just like in those beloved past times back home.

# CHAPTER VI

# Snake Handling for Amateurs

*"The danger of adventure is worth a
thousand days of ease and comfort."*

—Paulo Coelho

**THE ONE TOPIC** that never brought a smile to my parents' faces was my academic performance. From the youngest age, I was an all-star hooky player. There were far too many adventures to be experienced to successfully keep me idle inside dull, brick walls of a school all day. I knew there was nothing in that place that could compete with what I was learning in my life travels. *Nothing.*

On many mornings in Lynchburg, I'd leave my house with every intention of heading straight to school on my bike, but I'd get sidetracked on the way. The next thing I knew, I would just keep pedaling my red Huffy Sportsman bike far down a country road, or ditching the bike entirely to walk in the woods or alongside the railroad tracks. It's not a beacon of pride, but I confess: I had horrible grades throughout school. If I could not correlate an exercise or lesson to a sensorial experience or adventure, my mind would blank. If I came home with a "C" on my report card, my parents would go out to dinner to celebrate!

They tried all kinds of tricks and bribes to keep me in school, plus every sort of punishment just short of beatings and keelhauling like a sailor. They were exasperated, and I felt for them, but I couldn't reach them. I was just never able to take school seriously enough to attend it on any kind of regular basis. I still hold the record in the State of Virginia for the fact that no one, neither before nor after me, has yet to graduate from high school with one of their classes' final grades coming out to a "D," featuring 38 minuses. There'll be more fun stories on that later, though.

I remember one time when I was hitchhiking back from one of my train travels where I was picked up by the brother of Admiral Richard Byrd, the famed polar explorer. During the whole ride back to Lynchburg, he filled my head with stories about the Antarctic and North Pole. I probably didn't say three words, and by the time I stepped out of the car, I was practically an Admiral Byrd expedition expert. He had crossed the Atlantic Ocean, plus segments of the Arctic Ocean and the Antarctic Plateau. He claimed that his expeditions had been the first to reach both the North and South Pole by air. Admiral Byrd is also known for discovering Mount Sidley, the largest dormant volcano in Antarctica, in 1934.

It is only through such rich oral history and detailed stories from fellow wanderers (such as the brother of Admiral Byrd), paired with my ability to retain details and develop deep connections to people's life lessons they'd share, that

I am thoroughly convinced my years of skipping school were, indeed, the best thing I could've ever done to obtain knowledge which far transcended any traditional education that I would have received in school.

Doesn't that sound like a decent excuse for you, dear reader? By all local accounts, I was a good boy—just adventuresome.

If I had to lay claim to the most meaningful contribution that I made to any school during my childhood, it was my time as an eight-year-old snake catcher for a biology professor at Randolph-Macon Women's College in Lynchburg. I had been mowing and raking her yard for money because I'd always had an income-producing stripe. One day, she inquired, "Hey, I know you're out in the woods all the time . . . would you mind catching me some snakes for dissection in my class? I need as many as you can bring me."

She was offering $10 for poisonous and $5 for nonpoisonous; I had never heard of such easy money! I gladly accepted the position.

The next chance I got, I scurried to the local market and took a couple of burlap Idaho Potato sacks from the dumpster behind the store. From there, I headed to what seemed to be an ancient, abandoned shack in the middle of some woods that sat beside a creek. Its rusted tin roof had corroded into large tears and holes, and its wooden walls were dilapidated and moldy. On the wet, muddy floor lived more snakes than you could ever count; it had to be in the thousands– and most of them were copperheads.

If you're not familiar with copperheads, they're a venomous, reddish-tan pit viper native to the eastern United States. They can grow to be as long as three feet-plus and are as mean as they are ugly. They're known to hide themselves in dead leaves on the ground and strike at unsuspecting victims who step near them. Their venom usually isn't fatal to adult humans, but it *can be* in children (not that a train-hopping, school-skipping kid like myself cared much about risking death if it meant earning a crisp $10 bill). I could have found non-venomous snakes just as easily, but, given that they fetched only half the price, I didn't bother to look for any.

On warm days, some of the copperheads would leave the shack through the holes in the walls and sun themselves on exposed rocks along the creek bed. They were relaxed, basking in the sun's warmth, and practically comatose. As they rested, I would swing onto the large surface rocks from a nearby vine hanging from a giant oak tree, and precariously land on my trusty tennis shoes, making virtually no sound. As quick as lightning, I scooped my hand beneath a copperhead with my thumb on the back of its neck and threw it into the burlap sack before it even knew what was happening.

It may seem strange that a grown woman would have encouraged a boy to catch poisonous snakes, but the biology professor knew me well enough to know that I could handle myself in the woods. I spent a lot of time doing odd jobs for her and we got along swell. I was like the son she never had and my sense of humor always kept her laughing. She knew I was fearless – perhaps I reminded her of herself when young – so out of mutual respect for each other, we got along famously.

After bringing her bounties of copperheads for a while, she told me that she wished I would bring her some non-poisonous snakes, too.

"I'm sorry, ma'am, I just can't seem to find any," I explained.

"I know they're out there," she stated. "I see them all over the place. I bet if we go down to the creek, we could find one or two in the grass right now."

"Has it ever occurred to you that there's a sizable difference between a $10 bill and a $5 bill?" I retorted.

"Oh! I feel so stupid!" she said. "Okay, you're right. I stand corrected – all snakes are now $10!"

"In that case, I'll be right back!" I proclaimed.

Within a couple of hours, I showed up with my burlap sack full of vivid, green snakes and a couple of young king snakes to satisfy her biology lab's needs. From that point on, I attempted to give her equal portions of both poisonous *and* non-poisonous snakes.

The snake-seeking biology teacher wasn't the only neighbor who put me to work. The orphanage next door did too—they just didn't know they were doing it.

The Presbyterian Orphans Home in Lynchburg was built in 1911 and looked as much like a college campus as it did an orphanage. Occupying 1,000 grassy acres, its campus centered on a cluster of old Georgian Revival residence halls, a Greek Revival-style gym building, a swimming pool, and a domed executive building that looked like it belonged at Monticello or UVA. The orphanage was also a working farm, complete with a dairy barn, beef cattle, a stable and a farmhouse.

The kids who lived there worked the fields, grew the crops, and raised the cows, chickens, and pigs. For someone like me, it was a marvelous place to have in my backyard. Whenever I felt the urge, I'd climb through a hole I cut in the orphanage's barbed wired fence and join the kids for their chores. There were hundreds of orphans consisting of all different ages, so I blended in without a problem.

The orphans my age went to my school, so they all mostly knew me. At the end of the day, whether I was picking corn, helping milk cows, or doing whatever else was last required, it'd be time for the other kids to wash up and get ready for dinner, so I'd simply walk back down the hill and head home for the night.

My buddies at the orphanage were always amused by my visits. They'd laugh and joke with me for being there, and they appreciated the fact that I was sharing—with enthusiasm—what they thought was drudgery. The reason why I brought so much energy to the work there was because I knew I could stop and leave at anytime. They, on the other hand, couldn't. Also, I always found a certain amount of satisfaction from a hard day's work, especially when those labors involved helping others.

However, what I enjoyed most about the Presbyterian Orphans Home was actually its swimming pool. If you've never been to Lynchburg in the summer, let me tell you, it can be hotter than a billy goat madded by a blow torch! That spacious, big and beautifully blue swimming pool was my salvation on steamy days during summer months. I'd spend hours there, splashing around with other kids, with no one of authority knowing (or caring) that I was out of place.

Because the kids at the orphanage knew how I entered and exited the property, some of them would ask me to help them escape from time to time. They'd say things like, "I was separated from my brother or sister when I came here. I'd love to go see them."

My first response would be, "Well, do you know where they are?"

If they did, and the location was somewhere relatively

close in state like, Portsmouth for example, I'd tell them to meet me early on a designated morning, and then, at the appointed time, walk them to my jumping spot located near the train trestle. Normally, I wasn't one to encourage others to potentially get into trouble, but if I was tasked with helping reunite a family, I'd be more susceptible to influence than someone, such as my orphan friends, to do something riskier than they were used to.

"Okay, there's an eastbound train coming at noon today," I'd say. "It's headed Portsmouth's way – you just hop on. It'll be going slowly as it leaves the trestle. You can't miss."

Then, I would inform them of what to expect, wish them good luck, and be on my way. I felt deeply empathetic for some of these kids who were miserable about being apart from their family, so I had no choice but to help when I knew deep down that it was the right thing to do.

By now, you're probably thinking that I was quite the free spirit when I was a kid due to the number of times I stayed away from home, hopped trains, skipped school, and helped friends along the way to find lost loved ones. I guess I was just born that way, but I never intended, nor, to my knowledge, did I ever cause any harm.

I have always had a sense of joy helping other people. Whenever help was mixed with a strong sense of adventure, my thirst for drinking from the cup of human and worldly experiences served me well, particularly during my high school years—years that would bring seismic changes to my life.

# CHAPTER VII

# Wheels to Wonders

*"Earth and sky, woods and fields, lakes and rivers, the mountain and the sea, are excellent schoolmasters, and teach of us more than we can ever learn from books."*

—John Lubbock

**MY FREE-SPIRITED TENDENCIES** didn't fade in high school. Rather, they became more refined instead. At age sixteen, my mode of transportation graduated from hitchhiking, ride-sharing, and hopping in and out of older friends' cars, to driving my own self-purchased car a hair's breadth after I was old enough to legally get a driver's license. I got a car – a nice one at that – but how I scored the car is a story in itself.

I wasn't attending school very much at the time, but I was by no means lazing about. Upon turning fifteen, the age the State of Virginia allowed work permits for minors, I told my mother that I wanted to get a job, so she suggested I talk to the State of Virginia Employment Office to see what was available.

"They have jobs," she said. "That's what they're there for."

I called the Virginia Employment Office and a woman's voice answered. I said, "Do you have any jobs for a minor?"

"Are you crazy?" she asked.

"Not that I'm aware of. Why?"

"There are no damned mines in Lynchburg!" she exclaimed, thinking I was a miner.

The mistake was easier to make than you might realize. On the other side of the Blue Ridge, all the way up to West Virginia and into Pennsylvania, the countryside was filled with coal mines. Teenage boys had no problems finding a job if they didn't mind going deep into the earth and filling their lungs with coal dust. Thank goodness there were no mines near Lynchburg, or—given my enthusiasm for bringing home a hard-earned income—I probably would have found myself carrying a pick ax and wearing a helmet. Instead, the only coal to be found in Lynchburg came piled high in the passing train cars.

So, at age fifteen, I got a fairly high-paying job working the 4:00 p.m. to midnight shift at a local bakery. I caught loaves of bread as they came off the assembly line, put them on trays, and loaded them onto tractor-trailer trucks that then delivered the goods to grocery stores in the area.

No one questioned or even asked my age because I stood six feet tall, could grow a five o'clock shadow by noon, and was blessed with a face that looked ten years older than I really was. It's funny how, now that I'm more advanced in age, the opposite is true: I can look ten years younger than I truly am simply by shaving that (now-white) five o'clock shadow daily.

On hot days and nights during shifts at the bakery, I

would take my breaks in the cost accountant's office, which was the only air-conditioned room in the building. The cost accountant was the person who kept track of how many loaves of bread, rolls, honey buns and other items that were produced each day. He accounted for which trucks they were loaded onto, and where they all were sent.

This cost accountant's name was Buddy Rowe, and he was not only great with numbers, but also an amazing storyteller. Before settling in Lynchburg and working for the bakery, he divulged to me that he used to be a real-life spy. He spent time all over Europe, even in Russia, and was employed by American intelligence services.

I'm pretty skilled at spotting bullshitters, and I felt like he was telling the truth. No one else around the bakery believed him, though. This was around the time when James Bond was becoming popular with a new movie per year, and his stories were so similar, everybody else just thought he was spinning spy yarns for attention. After a while, I became his singular fan and target audience. When I would have a fifteen-minute break and spot him in the break room, I'd corner him and entice him to tell me another story, or simply finish the last one – the one where he was pinned down in Moscow, Warsaw or wherever. At times when he wasn't on break and I had a few free minutes, I'd walk into his air-conditioned office and shoot the cool breeze with him. However, Sam, my foreman, was always barging in, breaking up the conversation at fifteen minutes and ten seconds in.

"Okay, now it's time to get back to the floor," he'd announce. "You can't sit in the goddamn air conditioning all day," Sam would say as he did his best to sound aggravated (but never really was). Besides, I was a productive worker; Sam could never get too angry with me.

One day, Buddy went nose-down in his coffee at his desk from a sudden, fatal heart attack. (Admittedly, I always thought the KGB caught up to him to silence his storytelling.) I wasn't on the job that day, but the guys who were there told me that the ambulance attendants zipped him up in a plastic bag and rolled him out of his air-conditioned office on a gurney.

A couple of days after Buddy's death, I was working my shift catching bread on the factory floor when Sam's voice boomed over the loudspeaker, forcing everyone – even the conveyor belts – to a dead halt. He spoke to us from his glassed-in office which stood about thirty feet above us. When he was up there, he looked like God, or at least the owner of a football team surveying the field from his luxury box. To that point, I had never seen anyone walk up the stairs to his office besides him.

"Listen everybody," he stated. "We're going to have a few moments of silence for Buddy Rowe."

All of the workers on the floor watched Sam through the glass. He nodded, and we took the cue to spend a few minutes reflecting on old Buddy. It was a brief, but touching moment. Afterwards, Sam signaled for us to return to work by finishing with, "By the way, anybody who'd like to apply for Buddy Rowe's job, come up and talk to me. We want to hire from within."

My friends at the bakery, who all assumed I was 18 or older, started nudging me, saying, "Guy, go on up there. Go on up those stairs and get that job!"

At that time, my high school guidance counselors had decided in their infinite wisdom that I wasn't college material and placed me in a non-academic track called "distributive education." Its aim was to teach students a trade they could pursue after earning a high school diploma. I was hopeless in most of the classes, like home economics and welding, but there was one class that clicked for me: bookkeeping. The way of numbers made sense, and though I didn't attend class often, I still excelled.

After what must have been the 20th person on the factory floor that day who told me to go "get that job," I thought, *I have been taking that bookkeeping course, and what Buddy was doing seemed pretty easy . . . Besides, what's the worst Sam can do but throw me down the stairs?*

The next thing I knew, my legs were carrying me right up to the foreman's office. I opened the door, and there was Sam, sitting at his desk. He looked like Johnny Cash, wearing his regular set of black jeans and black shirt, with his black boots resting on the desk. He had worked his way up to this lofty perch after spending many long years doing every job in the factory and was as tough as they came. He would scrap with anybody who crossed him—in the bakery or on the truck line.

As foreman, I think Sam felt it necessary to show that if he was pushed, he could be meaner and tougher than the next guy. It was part of his mystique. Everybody loved him though, and at times, he could flash a sense of humor so warm it could melt a steel beam.

When he saw me at the top of the stairs, he motioned for me to walk in, sit down, and then growled, "What took you so long?"

"What do you mean?" I asked.

"Buddy Rowe and I talked about how when it was time for him to retire, that you'd be the perfect one to take over for him."

"Well, Sam, that's great," I said. "Does that mean I've

got the job?" He nodded. "I really appreciate it!" Just. Like. That.

He held up his hand to silence me and frowned. "There's a bigger reason why we're giving you the job."

"What's that?"

"You're the only one around here who's literate!" he bellowed with a smile.

He wasn't kidding. I won the job because I could read and write (not that I cared). At age sixteen, I was about to start earning an annual salary of $25,000 working the 4:00 p.m. to midnight shift as a cost accountant. The teachers at my high school were only making about $21,000 a year; I was about to be sitting in tall cotton! The whole situation seemed ridiculous, but I had a ball with it. *That* is how I ended up deciding to buy a car the second the ink dried on my newly issued paycheck at the ripe old age of 16 years old. It wasn't just any car, either. It was a 1967 green Ford Mustang. Convertible. Flashy. Spectacular. The perfect vehicle for so many lush escapades to come.

Between school, my adventuring, and my work at the bakery, I had begun to spend less and less time at home, and my parents stopped trying to keep track of me altogether (although they generally knew how to find me).

Given that I looked old for my years and the drinking age in Virginia was eighteen, I spent a good bit of time having fun at the local bars, making many older friends and enjoying the occasional dalliance with students from the nearby girls' college, Randolph-Macon. I relied heavily on my older looks, and though many of the bartenders suspected I was underage, luckily, they liked me and continued to serve me without challenge anyway.

The best of my drinking buddies were three West Virginia boys, whose names were Teddy, Billy and Eddie. They were renting a small terrace apartment together about a block from my favorite bar, the Cavalier. We got to know each other pretty well over a brief period of time and copious pitchers of beers. The trio was having great luck with the freshman women, as was I, so we had a lot in common. Successfully finding friendly company amongst the girls at the Cavalier became heaven-on-earth for a young man coming of age . . . *like me.*

It wasn't before long that the West Virginia boys began letting me crash at their apartment as a roommate, and I began spending far more nights there than at my parents' house. The apartment soon became my home; a very *Animal House*-style motif, long before the moviemakers ever thought of the concept.

One night, the four of us took a group of Randolph-Macon girls to the only upscale, fairly fancy nightclub in town named Nights Gallery. I went up to the bar to order drinks for the table—seeing how I had a bit more spending money due to my recent pay increase— someone pointed at me, singling me out, and informed the bartender by saying, "Hey. This guy's not eighteen. Card him!"

The bartender obliged, and I wasn't carrying any ID but my own. The bouncers escorted me, red-faced, from the establishment. One of the West Virginia boys saw how I was leaving the bar and ran out after me.

"What in the hell is going on?" he asked.

"Well, I'm not eighteen, and I don't have an ID that I can use."

His jaw dropped so far and so fast that it almost left a dent in the ground. He had no idea I wasn't eighteen (nor did any of my other apartment mates), so he went back into the nightclub and quietly told the rest of the guys about my situation—they couldn't stop laughing.

Not wanting to leave me on the curb, they left the bar and all of us, dates included, went back to the apartment. There, we drank like fish and played loud rock-n-roll music partying without worrying about legal ages or identification until the Randolph-Macon girls had to return to their dorms before curfew. By the time I went to bed that night, I was so inebriated that I couldn't see straight.

The next morning, the hammering in my head woke me, and I peeled my eyes open feeling lower than a snake's belly in a wagon rut. To work off the hangover, I trudged over to the lunch counter of a drugstore where I once worked as a part time soda jerk and ordered some bacon and eggs. I looked through the plate glass window as I sat there and noticed an old acquaintance, named James, who was at the gas station next to the drugstore. He stood there in a blue uniform, looking like something you would see in "Mayberry R.F.D."

That sight picked me up more than the plate of bacon and eggs did because I hadn't seen James in such a long time. He had been a fixture at that gas station when I was growing up, so after I paid the check, I walked over to say hello.

"Hey James. Good to see you. Where you been?" I asked.

"I had to go to Vietnam," he told me.

"You're kidding me. Tell me about it," I said, using the conversational skills I had mastered on so many car rides back from my train adventures.

Given that it was a Sunday morning there in the buckle of the Bible Belt, the streets of Lynchburg were empty. James had no customers, so we pulled up a couple of lawn chairs out in front of the station and talked. The conversation lasted a few hours, and I mostly listened as he recounted his jungle combat experiences. It was riveting. Toward the end, I told him what I was doing at the drugstore and how I got kicked out of the nightclub the evening just before. Once I finished, he said, "Well damn, boy, if you want to, you can take my identification," and he handed me his whole wallet.

Inside was his driver's license, draft card, library card, and an Ace Hardware receipt with his name on it– and, during that day and age, none of these IDs had pictures on them. James was over twenty-one years old: the legal age you needed to be in order to buy liquor in Virginia. For beer, you only had to be 18 . . . I had just hit the jackpot! I purposely haven't told you his last name until now. It was "Fortune." Perfect, right?

For years afterward, I became "Jimmy Fortune" whenever the moment suited me—mostly when I wanted to buy alcohol. I'd walk into one of the State of Virginia's ABC liquor stores around town from ages sixteen to eighteen, and clerks got to know me. When I'd walk in, they'd say, "How's everything, Jimmy? How's the family?"

I'd reply, "Great! The kids are growing up so fast, getting into trouble all the time," or something like that.

I used Jimmy's ID often and would hardly ever need to be anyone but myself due to small-town recognition. One simple flash of the ID, and I'd be known to be of age thereafter. With this newfound liberty, coupled with my tremendous income source and sense of adventure, I began breaking even further away from my parents and spending increasingly more of my time with Teddy, Billy and Eddie.

The apartment I shared with the West Virginia boys was

only a one-bedroom terrace apartment, but we all squeezed into it without any problems. We slept wherever we could find space on a given night. Usually, two of us would fit into the bedroom, and the other two crashed on a queen-sized hide-a-way pullout bed in the living room that doubled as a sofa. Or there was always the floor as a last resort. If anyone needed privacy with, say, a Randolph-Macon girl in the bedroom, that man was automatically granted the bed without question.

Every so often, I'd go to my parents' house about a mile away to do my laundry, say hello, or to grab a free meal. They really didn't realize I wasn't living there because they were accustomed to me not being around. In the past, I often stayed with friends or spent the night at the "clubhouse" that some of my buddies and friends had "remodeled a shack" in the woods and that always seemed to tie off the subject nicely. They certainly didn't know about the apartment or the hectic party schedule I was keeping with the West Virginia boys.

Our regular schedule called for the four of us to hit the bars Saturday and Sunday nights. Monday through Friday, I had the late shift, so my nights were unavailable for the most part. Teddy, Billy, and Eddie were great childhood friends. They had all graduated from White Sulfur Springs, West Virginia High School together and then came to the big city—which is what they considered Lynchburg to be because it had more than one stop light—to sow some oats before returning home to settle.

Eddie, for instance, was from a long line of pulp wood loggers, like his father, grandfather, and great grandfather before him. The guy was superhuman, which you need to be if your family profession involves walking into a forest, finding a 100-foot-tall tree, and sawing it down. Teddy was the nicest guy in the world and comedian of the group. Billy was a John Denver look-alike and had that same type of mild-mannered personality.

Together, we spent most of our time at the Cavalier, which was "the" college bar a short walk from the apartment. It's still in business today in the same weathered brick building, with the same giant plate-glass windows and ancient wooden booths where you can still sit inside and enjoy a hamburger or cold beer. In fact, the walls are still decorated by license plates and college banners, continuing its reputation of being a favorite haunt of Randolph-Macon students to this day.

Whether sitting in those booths or at the bar in the Cavalier, we were fortunate to meet many college girls who shared the same age restlessness as us. They were trying to forge a new path for themselves and escape from the bonds of family and restricted youth, no different from me or the West Virginia boys. It's true that we had a lot of fun partying with those girls, but I think there was a deeper connection that many of us failed to realize back then.

I can say with conviction that my middle teenage years were the start of a party for me in my life that has still never ended, and I hope never will end. I kept working at the bakery, making more money than King Croesus, and occasionally attending high school. Meanwhile, my guidance counselors kept me on the non-college, distributive education track.

I remember one of the guidance counselors telling me my sophomore year, "I think the greatest potential you have is as a sanitary engineer."

That was the nicest way for her to say that I wasn't

qualified for anything other than being a garbage man. I remember telling my mom about it, knowing that she'd have an adverse reaction for the speaker of those words at the high school. She was fearless, and though she had a golden sense of humor, she could turn into an angry mama bear at the drop of a hat if someone didn't treat her boy well. She took swift care of the matter, and my guidance counselors never suggested a career path for me again, nor, for that matter, did they ever see me again.

Since both of my parents had college degrees and their parents before them did as well, they were frustrated by my lack of interest in academics, but they got tired of trying to hammer a nail into a rock and eventually stopped pestering me about it.

Distributive education students were expected to show up at school at anearly time, like 9:00 a.m., but they were let out at noon every day so they could go to a job or apprenticeship that could lead them towards their future trade. They would earn graduation credits for the job if the place was approved by the school.

The setup was perfect for me. I told one of my teachers who knew me and my family well what I was doing at the bakery (and how much I was getting paid), so he made *sure* I was given plenty of slack by the school.

"You're doing something right, just keep doing it," he encouraged me. How could other teachers argue with him, especially considering the fact that I was making more money than they were?

In exchange for giving me more independence than most other distributive education students, he would ask me to sit down from time to time and regale him with numerous stories of my exploits. He was a mid-20-something bachelor that somewhat shy, so he liked living vicariously through me, thus I obliged. We became close friends. I miraculously received high enough marks from him to just barely cancel out my below-water grades and keep me from flunking out. Even though I was enrolled in a curriculum meant to prepare me for life beyond the age of 18, I hadn't given my future much thought. A game plan didn't seem necessary because everything always had a way of working out, whether it was finding a ride home from my train hopping or landing the highly sought cost accountant job. To me, my existence in high school was mostly about wine, women, and song. If there were more to life, I wasn't buying it!

# CHAPTER VIII

# Guy and the Girls

*"I feel the need to endanger myself every so often."*

—Tim Daly

I'VE LOVED THE company of women from the time I was smaller than a tadpole in a trout pond. The name of my first crush was Judy Farley. The two of us were in kindergarten and would sit next to each other in class and hang out together on the playground during recess. Bigger boys would hassle me for my adoration of her.

During my high school years, it was the age of countless love songs like the Beatles' "I Wanna Hold Your Hand" and "All You Need is Love," and I was drawn to the romance just as much as everybody else was. This is the main reason I enrolled in my high school choir class, held every Tuesday and Thursday. Previously, I had been a member of the church choir as a kid, with a decent voice, and was one of the few baritones among mostly sopranos and altos in the group. In other words, there weren't many boys in the choir class. Fortunately for me, many of the girls who had enrolled were quite attractive.

The teacher's name was Mr. Harris, and he was like a hotheaded cartoon character of a man who quickly grew to despise me. I was the Road Runner to his Wile E. Coyote, and, like the Coyote, he kept ending up with an anvil landing on his head.

At the start of the term, everything between the two of us went smoothly enough, but I soon became more interested in sneaking off with the girls in class than actually participating. As I got better acquainted with my fellow choir members, skipping into a nearby vacant room with them became pretty easy.

At first, Mr. Harris didn't seem to mind so much if I was absent, but over time, he started to realize that every time I, one of the baritones, was missing a class, so was an alto or soprano also missing. Usually, that missing alto or soprano and I were secretly two rooms down the hall playing our own steamy song. Eventually, he discovered the truth by interrogating one of the girls in the class and extracted information that then used as fuel for when the duel between he and I began. One by one, he took each of the choir girls aside and told them that an absence meant an *F*. Now, that hurt.

His strategy worked; the choirgirls stopped skipping class with me. I was not a happy camper anymore and all but entirely stopped attending class. He failed me for the course. When it came time to graduate at the end of my senior year, I realized that this *F* stood between me and graduation. I needed assistance, and it looked like Mr. Harris was going to have the last laugh. Enter Uncle Bob Bailey.

He wasn't really my uncle. He was the dean of men at

the high school, but also as close to any authority figure as I had in my life outside of my parents. He took a shine to me early on. I used to get into hot water for all kinds of crazy stuff—usually related to leaving the school grounds when I was bored, or when the weather was wonderful. Out of respect for my mother, who was so well-known and admired within the school system, no one suspended me. Instead, they sent me to Uncle Bob.

For instance, one of my favorite things to do was to check into the infirmary on the second floor, telling the nurse I was sick. Then, when no one was looking, I'd climb out the window and shimmy down an iron drainpipe to leave for the day. On the rare occasion when I would get caught, I found myself being told to report to Uncle Bob's office.

"Oh no, what did you do this time?" he would ask when I entered, barely looking up from the work on his desk.

He and I then negotiated on the number of detention hours I would receive. He'd say ten for almost everything and then we'd negotiate it down so I could complete the total detention hours due before the age of forty. I'd always remind him neither of us would live long enough to see them all served! He was a great guy and would *always* succumb to my math skills with a well-intentioned warning not to do these things again. The teachers who lacked a sense of humor for my antics, like Mr. Harris, complained to him all the time, but Uncle Bob just brushed it off. When I discovered that the "F" on my report card was going to keep me from graduating though, I was the one doing the complaining.

"My God, there is *no way* you're not going to graduate," Uncle Bob told me confidently before promptly leaving the office to speak with Mr. Harris.

As I later learned from eyewitnesses while waiting in Uncle Bob's office, the two men had a real knock-down, drag-out, shouting match in the choir room. It lasted quite a while, but once it ended, Uncle Bob returned to his office, thrusting my report card toward me.

"Look here," he urged. Your choir grade had been changed from an "F" to a "D" with thirty-eight minuses. "I said you'd graduate, didn't I?" He smiled.

Wile E. Coyote had once again fired his cannon, but the Road Runner lived to run another day. The next week at graduation, my parents cried. They couldn't believe that I had actually graduated with a diploma because the odds seemed so stacked against me ever getting out of high school. Given that my surname starts with a "V," I was one of the last kids to walk across the stage, and when I did, it was one of the happiest moments of my mom and dad's life. I could hear their tears of joy from all the way up in the balcony.

Uncle Bob was a constantly kind figure in my high school days. He was also the person who told me after my first junior year that I had to complete 11th grade again, which would move me from the class of 1971 to the class of 1972.

My first response was, "Why? I've just done the junior year thing."

"Well Guy, you can't attend only thirty out of 180 school days in a year and expect to advance to the next grade," he said.

"I guess I see your point," I shrugged.

Repeating my junior year ended up working out well for me because it gave me the chance to meet my future wife, a member of the class of 1972. I first saw her one morning before homeroom. I had already been living with the West Virginia boys in the apartment for quite some time and was knee-deep with college girls, but when I spotted her walking down the hallway, cheerleading baton in-hand with long, blond hair bouncing on her shoulders, I thought, *Holy shit, who is that?*

In the eyes of a seventeen-year-old, red-blooded American boy, she was hot perfection dressed in a majorette uniform. I was stunned. She passed with two other girls, and I collected my wits just in time to follow her for a short distance. The three made a path down the crowded hallways into the band room, where the band and cheerleaders were gathering. It was the biggest room in the high school and tiered like an amphitheater. The conductor's stand sat at the very bottom, in the center, and seats for the various sections of instruments rose around this focal point on different tiers. There were about eight levels altogether.

I entered the room just behind the girls and stood in the doorway on the side to watch. Sharon began speaking to a boy who I recognized from my second-period class. *Perfect,* I thought, *I've got a source for information!*

I stood for a short while longer, watching her, and became completely smitten. It was that magic moment when—if you're ever lucky enough to experience it— Cupid's arrow strikes you so hard that you nearly fall straight on your face. On my way out, I asked a kid in the room, "Who's that blond girl up there?"

He replied, "Oh, that's Sharon."

*Sharon.* I had a name . . . *Sharon.* First period moved slower than a drunk snail in cold molasses, and when second period finally arrived, I cornered the boy who had been talking to Sharon in the band room.

"Hey, I saw you with Sharon this morning. What's her story?" I asked.

"Why?" he replied.

"What do you mean, 'Why?'" I continued. "What's her story?"

The band kid understood what I was getting at and shook his head. "No way. There's no way," he whined in distress, as if I were planning to rob the Hope Diamond – Le Bijou du Roi; Le bleu de France; the Tavernier Blue – also known as one of the most famous diamonds in the world- from the Natural History Museum. "There's no way you could ever get Sharon! My God, man, her boyfriend's the captain of the football team!"

"So what?" I asked. A little, old boyfriend didn't seem like such a big obstacle to me.

"If you make one move toward her, you'll have the whole football team on your ass. There's no damned way!"

Well, if you ever want to light a fire under my rear end, just utter those four words: "There's no damned way." I was suddenly more motivated than ever to get into the good graces of Goddess Sharon. After some detective work, I discovered there was a girl we both knew in common, so I swiftly approached our mutual friend.

"Hey, you're friends with Sharon, right?"

"Yeah, she comes over to my house all the time, spends the night."

That was all I needed to hear. "Let's have lunch together in the cafeteria today. I want to know all about her," I said.

The two of us spent a half-hour at the cafeteria, and I got the entire background on Sharon, down to her favorite color and her "crazy-in-love" affection for the high school quarterback. The guy was practically Captain America—he was tall, with chiseled features, dark hair, and a scholarship to play football at North Carolina State, which was a big deal. Hell, I admired him too after listening to the details. Toward the end of the lunch, my informant provided one last piece of crucial information on Sharon, "She likes to play tennis." *Bingo, baby!*

I didn't have the opportunity to meet Sharon right away because work, life, and partying quickly took priority as summer vacation began, but she never left the recesses of my mind. Finally, not long before the end of summer vacation, prior to my second junior year, I decided to venture down her street in Lynchburg.

The fates were kind to me that day: she happened to be standing on the edge of her front yard mowing the grass, so I pulled beside her in my car and introduced myself.

"We have a mutual friend, Cathy," I said, "and we got to talking before the end of the school year. She said you're a tennis player."

"You're a tennis player, too?" Sharon said.

"Oh yeah, I love tennis. We ought to play sometime."

"Okay," she said. "I'd like that." Victory was mine, and it was sweet! We met three days later at some close-by local courts. After a pleasant match under the sweltering summer sun—I don't remember who won—we lingered and talked like old friends. She told me how her boyfriend had broken his leg running track, and was in a cast up to his hips, and how her summer had been miserable because of it. *We're going to be playing a lot of tennis,* I thought. Sharon also confided that the quarterback wasn't so nice to her, which didn't surprise me at all. It seemed he had a reputation of being the kind of guy who thought the sun comes up just to hear him crow. I, on the other hand, was always the opposite. I never found the need to be a great self-promoter because it never bodes well in any context. Our tennis-playing continued, and, not long after that first tennis outing, we finally fell for each other.

During the early stages of our courtship, I learned that I needed to change my ways a little to keep in her good graces. She only went with me to the West Virginia guys' apartment once and didn't like it at all. Sharon was smart enough to realize what went on there and didn't want any part of it. Because I was so smitten, I found myself spending less and less time at the apartment and continuously more time with her. I'd still sleep there, but when it was time for the gang to rally at the Cavalier, I didn't join them as often anymore.

The biggest obstacle our relationship faced was her parents. They didn't like me very much. Whenever I'd pick Sharon up at her house, her parents would frown. They knew their beautiful, smart, funny, and athletic daughter had what every boy desires and they looked at me as just any other boy. They didn't give a rat's ass about my wheels, gainful employment, easeful nature, polite manner, or adoration for their daughter (not that they would have liked anybody). Seeing her in any type or kind of a relationship was simply not desirable to them. Though I was older in terms of experience, she and I were technically only eight months apart in age.

Once, Sharon's old man even went to the length of filing a restraining order against me. I couldn't go within one hundred yards of his daughter at any time. *But how was he going to stop me? Or his daughter?* We were fatally smitten with one another. Forbidding us from being together only made our interludes more exciting. If we were having relations twice a day before that restraining order, we upped the ante to four times a day afterward.

The two of us made a plan that as soon as the clock struck midnight on her eighteenth birthday, we would run off together and life would be perfect. In the meantime, we were set on having as much fun as possible—which usually meant fooling around early, often, and everywhere, including at the high school itself- specifically, the top level of the high school library.

By far, the biggest room in Lynchburg High School was the library. It stood four stories tall. The first, and main, level contained the fiction and non-fiction sections and periodicals. The second level was the reference area. The third was more of an administrative level. And the fourth was for archived materials that you needed special permission to access. Almost no one ever went up there except for the librarians themselves to file new books or papers.

One day, I discovered that you could get into the fourth level through a door in an upstairs classroom—if you happened to know how to jimmy locks the way I did. I put the information in my memory banks, unused, until the newly-rebellious Sharon and I began looking for more creative places to have fun together. The library's fourth story became our secret love nest, especially after the school's final bell rang. We kept the lights off and barely made a noise so we wouldn't attract attention. We were "archiving" our love!

One time, at the end of the day as we were in the height of passion and naked as jaybirds, the light flipped on in the room. We turned to see a librarian innocently wander into the doorway, looking for something. She looked up, spotted us, and screamed so loudly that people could hear her all four floors below.

We couldn't run out the back classroom-access door naked because we would have exposed ourselves, so to speak, to all the kids and teachers still around there. We slowly, calmly, dressed and walked out the main door on the fourth level, descended the stairs to the bottom floor past the checkout desk, and exited the library like nothing had happened. No one said anything to us, ever.

That was the only time we ever got caught in the act. Though, there were a lot of close calls, especially when I snuck into her bedroom through the window. Her parents would routinely check on her and knock on her bedroom door. Then it was a matter of rolling under the bed or jumping out the window. Those were wild times. If her dad had ever caught me in the house, he would have shot me. It was always cat-and-mouse—and, I must say, one of the best periods of my life.

On the day Sharon turned eighteen in January of our senior year, we moved into an apartment together, just as we had planned. We thoroughly enjoyed the thrill of living together at first, but early on a Saturday morning in March, Sharon woke me up and announced, "I'm ready."

At first, I had no idea what she was talking about. "Ready for what?"

"I want to get married."

"Okay, we'll get married, but please, I want to go back to sleep!"

"No, I mean today."

"If you let go back to sleep, we'll get married today," I snapped.

"Okay!" she said.

A few hours later, she shook me in bed. "You ready?" she asked.

"Ready for what?"

"Getting married!"

"No! You're kidding, right? You're not serious," I proclaimed.

"No, I mean it, we're getting married today or I'm gonna leave."

I could see the determination on her face. "Fine. Let's get married," I said. "I'm gonna marry you anyway, whether it's today or another day. I'm really in love with you– might as well be today."

Minutes later, I called Howell, one of my closest friends, and asked for his help. He was a good friend and always dependable in a pinch. When Sharon and I had the restraining order hanging over our heads, Howell often picked her up from her house and brought her to me. He reminded me that in Virginia, the marriage age was twenty-one, but in North Carolina, it was only eighteen.

"Do you know any place over the border where we could get married real quick?" I asked.

"Sure, Chapel Hill."

The drive to Chapel Hill was a straight shot from Lynchburg down U.S. 501.

It's a busy college town, home to the University of North Carolina, so we figured if we could get a last-minute Saturday wedding anywhere in the state, it would probably be there. With Howell as our chauffeur, we headed south on the two-lane highway. A short way into the trip he asked, "What about a ring?"

I looked at Sharon. Neither of us had thought about it yet. Howell pulled into the nearest jeweler, and I paid for the nicest ring I could get with the cash in my wallet. We reached Chapel Hill in the afternoon and found a minister at a small Baptist church who said he'd be willing to marry us—with a marriage license. Howell, Sharon, and I hurried to the town hall and bought one for $15, then returned to the church to begin the ceremony.

"Are you sure you're ready?" the minister asked. "You're young and you've got your whole life in front of you. Very often, this is a mistake." We explained that we were confident it was the right decision. He nodded, looking like he had just finished speaking to the deaf, and led us to the altar. With Howell as our witness—the minister took out a *Bible* and said the magic words. Then, we kissed.

Two months later, we walked across the high school graduation podium with diplomas in our hands, and me, smiling with my *D* choir grade (complete with thirty-eight minuses, of course) on my report card. Neither of us returned to our seats with the other graduates. Instead, I walked straight to my car in the parking lot and sat in the driver's seat listening to the Rolling Stones and the Beatles. About twenty minutes later, Sharon appeared, still in her cap and gown. She opened the passenger side door and took her seat as I turned the key in the ignition and revved the engine. We drove directly to Florida, straight to the jobs that awaited us at a massive new amusement park outside of Orlando called Disney World.

# CHAPTER IX

# The Business of Responsible Adulting

*"The purpose of life, after all, is to live it, to taste experience to the utmost, to reach out eagerly and without fear for a newer and richer experience."*

—Eleanor Roosevelt

**UPON TEARING OUT** of the high school parking lot, Sharon and I drove straight down to Disney World. We had already lined up jobs well before we left. She was going to be a waitress at one of the resort's restaurants, and I would work in the wardrobe department for a couple of months until the construction on the accounting offices was complete.

The transition to married life and adult working world was smoother than we could have imagined, and Disney was an exciting place to be at that time. The resort had just opened about eight months prior, in October 1971, and couldn't be staffed fast enough to operate up to capacity. Back then, they were one of the best employers in the country.

Our escape to Florida was supposed to be merely the first stop in Sharon's and my plan to work our way around the world. If our jobs worked out well, we'd then transfer next to Disneyland in California. From there, we'd jump to Hawaii and move job-to-job across the Pacific, probably to New Zealand and Australia, and then continue to Asia and eventually make our way throughout all other continents—except maybe Antarctica. The world truly was at our fingertips!

I saw us returning to the U.S. and being ready to settle down and start a family in a decade or so; we'd still be in our late twenties, with a lifetime of memories and experiences to share with our little Van Cleves. Who wouldn't wish for a captive audience of children and grandchildren to keep one's adventurous tales alive? Sharon and I both agreed to follow this dream . . . at least for a hot minute.

To me, with both of us now living in Orlando and things going so well at Disney World, our plan of working our way around the world was alive and kicking, all things going according to plan flawlessly.

However, secretly, there was a flaw—trouble in paradise. One night at dinner, Sharon brought up the idea of having a child. I had to remind her that we were only twenty years old, and having kids at our age wasn't the best idea to coincide with our current, long-term plan (that we both agreed *would* include creating a long, happy family life). These chats about children picked up momentum and gradually turned into discourses between common sense and hormones. As you might imagine, common sense got thrown out the window and hormones won. Ultimately, Sharon made the choice to go off the pill on her own accord but didn't inform me of her decision. Children by ambush is seldomly the recipe for a happy family though.

Around the same time, I had been given a promotion to the job of accounting manager at work. I was filling the role that of a close friend of mine, Jim Ingersoll, one of many math geniuses from NASA, had left empty. Jim was laid off from the space agency as a result of budget cutbacks and then took an opening at Disney, since the company was still absorbing people like a vacuum cleaner. The two of us got along famously, even though Jim could cover a wall with all of his diplomas, degrees and certificates, and I had barely received my high school diploma. One day, he informed, however, that NASA had just offered him a better job (with higher pay) to return, and he had accepted. His job was now mine.

Though I was happy for now the new job, and the accounting department was a tight-knit group, I missed Jim when he left. Every time a new hotel at the resort would open up, everyone in my office—about fifty of us—would go to its bar and celebrate with cocktails. It became a kind of tradition. Dick Nunis, the CFO of WDW (the Walt Disney World Company), would often join the group too and pick up the tab. At one of these get-togethers, shortly after I became accounting manager, he sought me out to compliment me.

"Everybody thinks the world of you, Guy. You're great at what you do, and we like your work ethic. We made the right guy the accounting manager," he said. His kind words made me happier than a clam at high tide.

A few months later, though, Dick walked into my office with a serious look on his face. "I've got some bad news," he stated frankly. "It's come to my attention that you don't have an accounting degree."

"Never said I did," I explained. "If you look at my application, it said I've got lots of experience, but I don't have a degree."

"Well, unfortunately, the accounting manager position requires a college degree," he said. "So, what I'm gonna do is put you back in your old position, where you did such a great job, and I need you to go to get an accounting degree."

Dick told me I could take classes at Orange County Community College, which was closer to my apartment than the office was. "Before you know it, you'll have your degree, and you'll continue on with your remarkable career in accounting."

I didn't know what to say besides, "Sure, Dick. Sounds like a swell idea."

Right after the conversation, I drove over to the community college where the admissions department explained that my high school grade point average was too low for me to be accepted. It turned out that the *only* community college in the country (or world) that would accept me with my low grades would be Central Virginia Community College that, by law, was required to take all Lynchburg students who had successfully earned their high school diploma.

So, it was back to the Old Dominion state for Sharon and me—and our baby, which was on the way. Sharon had quit her waitressing job, and I told Dick about the pregnancy, expressing how it'd be good for us to be near family while I tried to earn an income and become enrolled in accounting classes.

"Well, get that degree and come on back. You've got a job anytime you want it," Dick responded.

In Lynchburg, Sharon gave birth to our son, Charley, and I took a full-time job as a cost accountant for a company that made industrial air conditioners while also carrying a full course load at school. Our marriage was a whirlwind after that. I finished my two-year associate's degree in eighteen months, and the two of us became adjusted to life as new parents. Sharon took a job at the local A&P grocery store to bring in some extra money (and get out of the house some), while I escaped sometimes on the weekends with my buddy, Joe, to ride motocross in the Appalachian Mountains. He was a neighbor and a new father as well.

During this time, my relationship with Sharon grew strained. Our perspectives and priorities changed, and the divide between us had become a gaping hole that couldn't be filled. Our *own* Disney movie had come to an end. As days became weeks and weeks became months, our mounting, and now, many differences eclipsed what had brought us together. Sadly, we divorced. Sharon wanted sole custody of Charley, and for reasons that I wish to remain private for all parties involved, I agreed with her wishes.

With nowhere else to go after my breakup with Sharon, I turned to my friend, Howell (the friend who had driven me to the church on my wedding day). He was living in a small complex of singles apartments called Stratford Hall and working at the Pizza Hut on Bedford Avenue in Lynchburg. Howell kindly let me crash at his place, and I spent quite a bit of my free time hanging out at his restaurant in the beginning.

One Wednesday night at the Pizza Hut, I met a salesman about my age named Dusty. He was the kind of guy who gets to know everybody in a room, including their first name, faster than green grass goes through a goose. We became close friends in just a few minutes.

Dusty was from Atlanta and, during our conversation, kept singing its praises. To a red-blooded young man like me, the place sounded like a mix of Las Vegas, New York, and the Pearly Gates of Heaven, all wrapped up in a beautiful, Southern, peach-blossomed bow. As Dusty spoke, Howell gave me a nod and a look that signaled, "We're going there!"

I nodded back, and the following Saturday, the two of us plus a couple of other friends piled into my car, a Chevy Malibu that had replaced the Mustang, and tore down to Atlanta where we spent one rowdy-yet-tremendously-fun night hitting both the town and The Underground. While nursing our hangovers the next morning, I picked up the newspaper left at our door at the Marriott Hotel where were staying. It was so thick with pages, I had to grab it with two hands. The "Help Wanted" section alone was about three times bigger than the entire Sunday "Daily Advance" newspaper in Lynchburg.

My friends and I spent most of our seven-hour drive pouring through the job listings in that newspaper. After less than twenty-four hours in Atlanta, we had fallen in love with the place and decided we would return to live there permanently. Besides, it was time for me to put the sting of my divorce in the rear-view mirror. Howell and I, plus two others, made a solemn pact practically sealed with blood to move down to Atlanta, but when the day to finally make the big move arrived, only Howell and I actually did it.

Howell packed what few things he owned, like a bed and his stereo, into a U-Haul trailer, and I put the entirety of my belongings—little more than a couple of shirts, jeans, underwear, and a few pairs of socks—into the trunk of my Malibu, and off we went. To this day, Howell and I are still the closest of friends. We talk almost every week. Though we never saw the mysterious, charismatic Dusty individual again after that night in the Pizza Hut, he's the reason Howell and I still live in Atlanta to this day.

Upon our arrival, I got a job as an assistant manager at Kentucky Fried Chicken. It wasn't glamorous, but it did have its greasy benefits. At the end of every night, I'd take buckets of finger-lickin' leftovers home for Howell and new friends that we had made in the apartment complex where we first settled. There were about eight of us who became tight, fairly quickly. I had only been working at KFC about a month when the store manager was caught having an affair with a counter girl in the walk-in cooler at the back of the restaurant. The wife had found out, and he was gone quicker than a toupee in a hurricane. The district manager then approached me—maybe because I was the only employee who looked like he hadn't just come back from serving ten years at San Quentin—and said, "You! You're acting manager now. Come to the main office this week, and we'll teach you what you need to know."

I did what I was told and became manager of the Kentucky Fried Chicken restaurant, and, before I knew it, I had turned it into the most profitable store (out of sixty-three) in the district. Then, at the end of the summer of 1974, KFC offered me the job of district manager. The regional manager told me, "I'll offer you $100,000 a year and an Oldsmobile Cutlass company car if you take the position."

I was honored and thrilled. That salary was quite a chunk of change for someone my age too, but I turned it down. I decided it was time for me to finish my four-year college degree before I wandered too far into a career. It seemed that no one would take me seriously in the accounting profession unless I improved my credentials, and that I'd keep hitting dead ends (like how I did at Disney) otherwise. The regional manager asked me if there was anything that he could do to change my mind.

"Nothing," I replied. "I've got to go to the University of Richmond. It's where my father went, and I have to finish the last two years of my education. I feel like that's more important than $100,000 a year and a new Cutlass," I explained.

"Well, if you get to Richmond and you don't like it, you come on back down here. That's fine."

That fall, I enrolled in classes at the university in the town where I was born.

I had returned to Richmond, just as I had vowed to do when I was seven years old, but I wouldn't stay there long. The University of Richmond's School of Business was quite an impressive place for a country boy like me . . . talk about feeling like a duck swimming with a flock of swans! The professors were all Ph.Ds. from B.F.D. places like Wharton, Harvard, Princeton, and Yale. All of them seemed to have initials before or after their name—with some thrown in the middle for good measure—and my fellow classmates were incredible people who came from all around the world.

I met a fellow from the third-wealthiest family on the planet (who I'll call, "Third"). His family has owned the tobacco rights to Asia since Marco Polo had a cup of tea with the Emperor of China and pulled out a strange, little leather purse containing tobacco inside. His family had more Gulfstream jets than most people have shoes. On his apartment wall, he hung thirty-eight pictures of thirty-eight yachts his family owned around the world. I'm talking nothing under one hundred feet in length. Just amazing.

The person that I met Third through was the BMOC (Big Man On Campus), who also started his student living in the dorms, but now, as a senior, had moved off campus. During my first week of moving into my dorm room, several fortuitous things happened in rapid sequence.

I moved into an old dorm building with stately large, brick windows that opened, but no central air conditioning was in the building. When my assigned dormitory's door was opened by the third floor's student supervisor, he showed me the ins-and-outs, handed off the university's do's and don'ts booklet of dorm life to me, and then I asked him if we had any poker players in our dorm (I had been playing cards since learning how to sit in a chair without falling out). He replied that he and five other people had a semi-regular game down in his room and offered to put me on the invite list. The cast was set.

Within twenty-four hours, I installed a too-big-for-the-square-footage window air conditioner, just in case I wanted to monetize a hanging meat food locker later. I pushed the two twin beds together in such a way that would provide a double bed ride, then placed a new double bed mattress on the two as the cherry on top.

Thereafter, I pushed the two "study" desks together facing each other to make for one large, flat surface large enough to support a small but impressive roulette wheel that had accompanying felt, which was a perfect table fit when stretched a little and then hard Velcro'd down. Lastly, with this sizable empty space left over in the room (thanks to the efficiencies from *moi's* room design), a perfectly sized six-person card table was finished off with chairs, completing the vision for my new, full-service dorm casino.

First and second nights' selective invites confirmed that

it was a hit. A few quick-whispered grins among the cool-breeze hallway boys in this large five-story dormitory made it "the" place to stop after a full day of sweating over hard bound textbooks.

Just hearing something about textbooks broadened my interest to go buy a few. By the third day, I was off to the campus bookstore and during the first week or two of any new semester, the campus bookstore was frantic, if not panicked, by wide-eyed consumerism. Here, I bumped into a Lynchburg boy who I had grown up with. His father owned a large highway paving company and he lived pretty high on the hog back in our old burg.

His name was Mike, and we had a great, mutual "How the hell are you?" reunion. We swapped mostly current events, and beers, at the closest pub to round out our full catch-up session. Obviously, I invited him to my third invitational casino night.

While having a great time together, and with a little luck at the tables, Mike pulled me aside and said, "There is someone you must meet. His name is John. He is a senior like me and is unquestionably the BMOC." Never one to be shy, I said, "Sure."

Two remarkable things happened the next day. The first involved the fact that I always slept in late. Classes normally started at 8:00 a.m., and I would rise at about 9:30 a.m., so the 8:00 a.m. classes were not my best classes. However, today it was good to be "home" when there was a knock on my door at about 9:00 a.m. It was this collegiate, well-dressed, well-mannered, twenty-year-old black kid hailing from Philadelphia with suitcases in his hands.

With the door half cracked, I tiredly asked how I could help him. He stated his name was Bill and that he was assigned this dorm room, too. Suddenly, I remembered the room as I first entered it was configured for two. The dorm supervisor had said nothing to me about a roommate.

Then with the luck of twenty lottery winners, he stuck his head in the room enough to see the casino operations. Never having put his suitcases down, he turned to me and said, "It doesn't appear that you are here to be a serious student!"

I was awake enough now to feel the full import of his concern and replied, "Yeah, that could be somewhat of a fair observation." Bill made clear he was at college to exceed all academic expectations and that other housing may serve him well. I love it when everybody enthusiastically agrees about anything, so off Bill went to find another room with my best wishes for all his future academic successes.

Now that I was awake, I remembered that today was the day I was to meet Mike for lunch and go meet John BMOC. So, I took my time and missed another class, if you can imagine, to meet for lunch. Mike was already at a table at 11:30 a.m. when I walked in to the best burger and club sandwich joint near campus. After loud laughter, big burgers, and a couple of beers later, we headed off to John's Court.

John was both literally and figuratively everybody's best friend. He rented a mansion overlooking the James River that had an expansive party room, living rooms, large ter-races off the main living room and upper bedrooms, all together with a state-of-the-art, house-wide stereo befitting New York City's Studio 54.

Okay, first impression, he knocked down all my bowling pins. John stood about 6'1" and had a thick full mane of blonde hair with a kingly, stout figure and a smile that could charm even the downtrodden. Mike and John had been running buddies for years. To my great surprise, Mike's introduction of me was laced with his regaling John stories of my Randolph Macon Women's College high school exploits, which I had no idea he ever knew about. I guessed small-town gossip was still at play even years later.

I was immediately welcomed in as one of John's VIP party guests and ran with his small entourage over and through every happening night club and high-flying party circuit in Richmond, Virginia. And oh baby, the party lifestyle was alive and living in Richmond, Virginia!

Notables that were our age were the Reynolds brothers and who I will deem Third (from the third wealthiest family). The Reynolds boys were not students at the university, just constant partiers. There were two separate but distinct billionaire Reynolds families in Richmond. One was in metals/aluminum and the other in tobacco. All parties involved will thank me not to specify which one is the one that I speak of in these memoirs.

The Reynolds boys had a huge mansion, possibly once a plantation house on the banks of the James River. The sandy riverbank was a fabulous extension of the well-attended party house and grounds. I was only there when there was more than 100 well-favored girls and guys having the best of times, day and night, (and next day and night, so on and so forth). Every time we went to the plantation, there was a festival-style party already in full swing, and we'd crawl, knee walk, or get help being carried away each time we decided it was time to leave. I never saw one of these plantation festivals come to an end.

Ah, there is wealth, and then there is . . . *wealth*. John was good friends, no—strike that—John was Third's best friend in the entire Richmond scene. Meeting and hanging out with Third was quite memorable. Albeit no matter how frequent our visits, Third was friendly to me but could never be considered a friend. He and John were true friends, and in those days, that was good enough for me.

Then, there were the almost full-blur occasions. One night, at about 11:30 p.m., we ran out of everything and anything to drink at Third's crib. Having more than one Rolls, he picked the color of the moment and drove like a bat out of hell, with John in the front "shotgun" seat, plus Mike and me in the back. We all departed, destined to arrive at what was reasoned to be the closest liquor store before closing.

First one closed, second one closed, and then, maddened by this circumstance, John spoke of one some 10 or more miles away, but we would have to get on Interstate I-95. Two turns later, Third drove well over 100mph, not caring how the high-speed lane changes affected his backseat passengers. With all pupils dilated, we were breathlessly following wherever he was going, and everyone but Third wondered if all wills were in order. Next up, the Virginia State Patrol showed up, lights and sirens ablaze.

Admittedly, drunk, sober, or somewhere in between, all *passengers* were relieved. Third was kind enough to pull over and adopt his native Chinese tongue when the trooper really wanted to know where the fire was and politely asked for Third's driver's license. Not understanding a word out of Third's mouth, I did catch the trooper noticing that it was an international driver's license. The trooper asked Third to go sit in the back of his police car and, once that fiasco was settled, he returned to see what the hell was going on here after midnight, preferably in native English.

John was the first to assure the trooper that we were all just college buddies and – sobered by the "life in your throat" highway midnight chase for more booze– we assured him that there had been no drinking. He was so relieved at the sound of our use of English that he said the second police car, pulling up behind us, would take us somewhere safe off the expressway to catch a cab home.

We were escorted to the second State Patrol car, and off we went – no sirens or lights, just a most-welcomed, calm ride. Then trooper explained that he was needed back on the highway and was only good for a *short* ride, not intending to take us home or anywhere else. We were dropped at a "looks like a cab pick-up corner" and waited, waited, and waited some more. It became clear that no traffic on the streets meant that no cabs were coming, so with what adrenaline we had left over from our Rolls-A-Coaster ride, we walked, walked, and walked until Mike finally, literally, chased down a cab.

John's first concern was for whom to contact to help Third. We agreed and went to Third's place so John could start to figure out what to do next. To our surprise, Third was there, calmly watching TV. It turns out that he had diplomatic immunity, and once that was confirmed, he spoke English well enough to be given a ride home by the arresting officer. We sure learned a little bit about diplomatic immunity that night!

Lastly, and quite notably, was Third's rides to go out to eat mostly seafood– and really good Chinese food. He had a thing for a New York City Chinese restaurant and a seafood place in Miami. To ordinary humans, the local Richmond fare was sufficient. To Third, it was as effortless as picking up a television remote to arrange a private jet to go dining.

On those occasions, the party was in the ionosphere. As any and all young twenty-something-year-old lads, we had very healthy, wide-spectrum appetites. However, Third's handlers intimately knew all his appetites extremely well, and whenever it came time to board the jet (seldom ever the same jet twice), it was stocked with both a full bar and his culture's traditional assortment of concubines.

Never to be known as one to throw rocks at any man's cultural house, I was happy to support the traditions of the east. Each landing was met by red carpets and large limousines for just the guys to pile into, go to dinner, and then party after at a local favorite nightclub or two before the return trip home.

These episodes were the exception to our normal life. Rudely, weekday class attendance and self-sustaining income requirements mandated some form of repeating work routine for sustenance. Being true to my accounting roots, I found an amazingly forgiving (okay to be late or need exam (recovery time) off as a college student) job. I was a part-time accounting/coding clerk for a large interstate trucking outfit that mostly picked up and delivered from the Reynolds Metals and Aluminum manufacturing plants. Bills of lading and tariffed shipments needed placards on the trucks to match the freight bills. I was one of many coding clerks who prepared the paperwork to be delivered to the terminals being awaited by the drivers, they were then attached to the proper eighteen-wheeler's exterior markings. All went well and I couldn't ask for more as I thought there was no more real estate left on my plate during these crazy days.

Then the "never say never" opportunity popped up when me and a school buddy, over campus beers, decided our next ambitious move was to go into a promising business venture, later made famous by one of my favorite Burt Reynolds movies, "Smokey and the Bandit." Burt's character is a trucker hired by a business tycoon to bring 400 cases of Coors beer from the west to Atlanta. At that time, Coors was a regional beer, which couldn't be legally sold anywhere east of the Mississippi. As a result, it had an impressive cult following. That's right, Coors beer had a cult following!

I thought, *let's get Coors east of the Mississippi! Who the hell cares where the lines are drawn? Let's change those lines!*

I rounded up a few more guys from my B School classes who were budding entrepreneurs like me—but with the added advantage of generous trust funds in their names—and a few of the big money boys in our group sat down in Golden, Colorado with Coors executives themselves. Our groups worked out a plan to distribute their beer in the South. The work was time-intensive and diverted me from my schoolwork a bit . . . not that it affected my grades much, especially in my accounting classes.

Accounting is a subject that came naturally to me, even on that advanced level. As I sat in the lectures, I understood everything the professors were saying, intuitively. I'd flip through a textbook and say to myself, "This isn't anything much different than I've been doing since I was working at the bakery or Disney!"

I was acing the tests and working on the Coors venture, so I started going to fewer and fewer of the accounting lectures. One of my professors took exception to my spotty attendance record, though, and gave me an "incomplete" at the end of the fall semester. I went to his office to object, pointing out that I earned one of the top grades in the final exam.

"I don't care. I'm giving you an incomplete because you didn't sit in my classroom long enough to have fully completed the course," he stated adamantly.

"I respect what you're saying, but I'd like to hear this from a higher authority," I replied.

If I had a problem in high school, I always leaned on Uncle Bob, who understood me so well and was almost always willing to give me the benefit of the doubt. At the University of Richmond, however, I didn't know anyone in the administration personally.

I did know who to speak with though. His name was Dr. W. David Robbins, dean of the business school. The only authority higher than him to complain to was God, the Lord almighty, who wasn't returning my calls. Dr. Robbins was a larger-than-life figure on campus, the author of many renowned books and Harvard trained. He was on the boards of many large corporations and charities. He alone had the power to change my grade, and I was determined to see him.

I walked to the waiting area outside his office, where his assistant sat, and the place looked exactly like you'd expect from a fancy college; it had all dark mahogany furniture that looked more like museum pieces than something meant for people to actually use. I almost started looking for the velvet ropes to keep the commoners like me from touching anything valuable.

The secretary said Dr. Robbins wasn't in, so I said I'd wait for him. As I stood there, biding my time, I peeked through the open crack of his office door. It was even more magnificent than the waiting area. He had a massive desk that looked like it was hand-carved from a single virgin trunk of Virginia oak, and it sat on top of a carpet so thick and beautiful it would have made the one inside the Oval Office of the President of the United States look shabby. I was beginning to think that maybe Dr. Robbins and the Lord Almighty were one in the same.

After several minutes, the man himself breezed through the waiting area, looking straight out of Snooty College President Central Casting—from his doughy frame, to his thick glasses, to his impeccably tailored suit, all the way down to the perfectly starched and ironed handkerchief that you know will never, ever actually touch a human nose for the entirety of its existence.

As he passed, he shot me a glance. He knew I was there to see him, so he said to his assistant, without addressing me directly, "I'll be right with this gentleman, but if Dick Nunis calls, I want to be interrupted."

*Dick Nunis? Is that the same Dick Nunis, my friend at Disney?* It had to be. I realized at that moment that another door in my life was about to open, and I'd be a damned fool if I didn't walk through it. The secretary eventually told me that Dr. Robbins would see me.

Upon entering his office, I introduced myself and told him my situation. "I've got a little thing going on with one of my accounting professors. He took exception to the fact that I couldn't attend as many of his lectures as he would have liked, but I aced his exam and *all* of my other accounting exams for that matter. I would just like to talk to you about this."

Dr. Robbins peered down from the top of his glasses at me, looking skeptically. "What makes you think you aced the exam?"

"Well, I kind of knew all the answers," I said.

"And why did you miss so much class?"

"I've been involved in a business venture that's going to bring Coors beer east of the Mississippi, and it looks very promising. It's going to mean a lot to Richmond, Virginia. We're going to put the distribution facilities here, and it will bring a lot of jobs. The arrangement took a little more time than I would have liked, which took me away from my classes more than I planned."

"Oh, interesting," Dr. Robbins said.

While he may have been sincerely interested in the Coors venture, it wasn't enough ammunition to convince him to overlook the missed classes. I could see I needed to pull out the heavy artillery before he kicked me out of his office.

"Sir, I couldn't help but notice that you mentioned Dick Nunis."

"Yes. Why do you mention it?"

"Well, I know him."

"How is that?"

"I used to work at Disney." I explained that I was an accountant there and had gotten to be friendly with Nunis.

Suddenly, Dr. Robbins' whole demeanor changed. His perpetual frown turned into a friendly, let's-make-a-deal smile. He told me that he was working on a book on the "top 20 most successful business ventures that had been started from the ground-up" by ambitious and forward-thinking entrepreneurs. It would be used as a text for business school classes at colleges and universities across the country. "I've finished nineteen chapters, but there's one left: Walt Disney and the Disney Company."

As part of his research, he wanted to see the Disney World tunnels, which span miles and miles and connect most all the park's rides and food stands. They were built to allow performers, repair people, trash men, and even armored trucks carrying cash to travel from place to place in the park without being seen by the paying customers. Walt Disney himself thought that by keeping as much of the park's people and operations backstage, if you will, it maintained the magic and illusion of the Magic Kingdom.

The tunnels are called utilidors, short for utility corridors, and the wardrobe department—where I first started working when I arrived at Disney World—was located directly in them. "Oh yeah, I practically lived in those tunnels for a while," I said to Dr. Robbins, trying to keep a neutral professional tone while my mind leaped for the possibilities. "I had my own golf cart for getting around in them.

What do you want to know about them?"

"I'm familiar with them. I've read stories and talked to people, but I want to go inside them. I've gone up the chain of command, and everybody has told me that the only person who can give me access is Dick Nunis."

This was my golden chance! "Well, Dean, maybe I can help you if you help me," I proffered.

"What do you mean?"

"Well, if I get you that tour you want through the tunnels, can I get my grade in my accounting class adjusted to the *A* that I earned?"

"Absolutely!"

We extended hands and shook. Then I picked up the phone on his desk and called Dick Nunis' office directly. He had just been promoted to president of the park. Nunis' secretary transferred my call straight to him. *Mr. Good "Jimmy" Fortune, you still must be with me, buddy!*

"Hey Dick, this is Guy! How are you? . . . That's good

to hear! Yes, I'm fine, too. I'm at the University of Richmond in Virginia, getting my college education, just as I promised. I figure I'm about a year from getting back down to Florida."

We had a five-minute conversation, catching up and exchanging pleasantries as Dr. Robbins sat across his desk from me, waiting impatiently. Finally, I told Dick, "I want to introduce you to a friend of mine. His name is David Robbins, and he is writing the seminal book on how entrepreneurs created huge, wonderful corporations. It's going to be sold in every business school in America, and he just needs some special access and a little time and consideration."

Dick told me he'd be happy to speak to him. I handed the phone to Dr. Robbins, who had likely wet those tailored breeches of his. When the conversation ended, he told me, "Son, you've got your 'A' and my great gratitude".

I went home for Christmas break and never saw the man again. In fact, I never even returned to campus. The Coors deal fell through; however, I am convinced we played a pivotal role in Coors ultimately crossing the Mississippi. I couldn't go back because I was getting restless again to see the world. I had scored another semester's credit, but in my mind, time was wasting.

# CHAPTER X

# Volcanoes Over My Shoulder

*"The world is big, and I want to have a
good look at it before it gets dark."*

—John Muir

**WHEN I RETURNED** home for Christmas break from the University of Richmond, I felt like I was off schedule with my dreams to see the world. Every second that passed was another second wasted. My original plan was to work a couple of years at Disney, then go do the West Coast, then Hawaii, New Zealand, and keep wandering from there. My life's path had taken me in other directions though—through parenthood, divorce, and college. It was time for me to get back on that original track. My senses were jumping inside me to be met.

To make up for lost time, I decided to skip California and proceed directly to Hawaii. I had watched endless episodes of "Hawaii Five-O" and seen the movie "Endless Summer" more times than I could count on my hands and toes. It was time for me to be the leading man in my visions of that tropical island paradise. Hawaii, to me, symbolized a simpler way of life—and a place of exploration. It had towering volcanoes connected by winding, mountainous roads where I could ride my motorcycle and be the master of all I surveyed. It had surfing, constant sunshine, and blue water. I planned to play there a little bit, land a job to sustain me for a couple of years, then continue my round-the-world journey. I had no inkling nor notion that I'd soon be finding my way onto the world's largest luxury cruise ship not long after I'd arrive there (not that I would have been surprised to hear it). For me, the experience has always been more important than the actual destination.

Before I left for Hawaii, I returned to Atlanta to tell my buddies. None of them took me seriously, not even my best friend, Howell, who I had originally moved down there with. I made my final preparations, like unloading most of my worldly possessions and pre-ordering a Yamaha on and off-road motorcycle to be waiting for me in Hawaii upon my arrival. My last act was selling my bronze-colored 1972 Chevy Malibu, which I sold to a friend who lived across the parking lot from my old apartment building. He needed a new set of wheels, and I needed the money, so we signed the papers, he gave me a check, and then drove me to the bank to cash it. He then headed straight to the airport to drop me off ticket in hand!

I boarded the United Airlines jet in Atlanta with nothing more to my name than a small amount of cash, a few changes of clean clothes stuffed inside a small suitcase, and a motorcycle helmet. Soon after, I was crossing the Mississippi for the first time in my life at 30,000 feet in the air. It was a day of firsts as I looked out over the Great Plains, then the Rocky Mountains and finally, the Southwestern Deserts. I was happy as a fat tick on a fat dog.

Once I landed, there was a layover in Los Angeles –my first time setting foot in California– and then a flight over the Pacific. I held a steady eye out the window, with all the excitement and euphoria you could cram into one body without it bursting. I thought to myself, *I'm on the threshold of everything possible!*

Upon touching down in Hawaii, I stepped down the stairs leading from the plane's exit, blasted by the warm humid air. Beneath me was the bleached airport tarmac baking beneath the late afternoon sun. As my feet hit solid ground, a woman in a Hawaiian shirt draped a flowery lei around my neck. There's nothing quite like that feeling from the first time you get *lei'd*.

The airport scene seemed so familiar to me because I had watched it so many times on "Hawaii Five-O." I felt instant recognition, like I belonged in this place. I made the short walk to baggage claim and grabbed my modest suitcase when it appeared on the carousel and walked over to a set of nearby coin-operated lockers. I deposited a few quarters, opened one of the doors and placed my luggage inside. My actions were reflexive. I didn't have a plan, and I followed whatever action popped into my mind.

From there, I walked out of the terminal and hailed a taxi.

"Take me to the Yamaha dealer on Nimitz Highway, please," I told the driver upon settling into the back seat. Time to get that motorcycle.

The dealership was—and still is—located only a few miles from the airport, and I arrived shortly before closing. To my relief and incredible joy, the motorcycle was ready and waiting for me, custom-built with a few personalized touches, and with a registered Hawaiian license plate proudly hanging on the back. I signed the necessary forms and asked the sales-man, "Which way is the beach? Which way is Honolulu?"

He replied, "Go out our driveway and turn right. You can't miss it."

I pulled out of the dealership, and turned right as instructed and soon enough, Honolulu appeared before me. The ocean air was intoxicating. *Paradise abounds!* Then, I hit rush hour traffic. Nothing quite brings you back to reality like cars parked bumper-to-bumper on the road in front of you. Not that I minded too much because the sights and the air were so exotic.

Soon, I passed the lifeguard stands and crowds on cres-cent-shaped Ala Moana Beach Park, which houses one of the most popular stretches of beach on Oahu. The thought hadn't yet occurred to me that I would need a place to sleep that night, although it shortly would because the sun was setting.

I kept following the flow of traffic, stop-and-go, stop-and-go, as it took me through downtown Honolulu, passing alongside the towering oceanfront hotels. To my right, I eyed an unused lane of highway, completely free of traffic, as if it was invisible to the other motorists around me. I took this one road less traveled by and cruised past all the vehi-cles standing still. Freed from the traffic, I simply absorbed the sites for about a half-mile before I noticed a bus in my rear-view mirror, driving barely a possum's length from my back license plate.

I thought, *oh my God! What's going on? Why is this maniac riding my butt? Is he trying to kill me or something? What the hell?*

I accelerated, he accelerated, like we were in a high-speed "Hawaii Five-O" chase scene. To lose him, I ran through a red light. That's when I noticed the traffic sign telling drivers that the street's right lane was reserved for public transportation only. That bus driver was trying to send me a clear message to get the hell off his side of the road—even if he had to kill me to do it. I was charged higher than a hummingbird drinking from a honey pot with a straw. I had to pull off the road to reclaim composure.

After calming down, I realized I was in Waikiki, a beachfront retail business center in Honolulu, and spotted the Hilton Hawaiian Village, which to me at that very moment was a perfectly sculpted Eden, minus the snake. It had tall palm trees waving in the wind and cascading waterfalls flowing into shimmering ponds. It had swimming pools, tiki bars, and bungalows spread beneath the main hotel tower. It sat along a sugary beach, glowing in artificial light as the sun set. I'd never seen anything like this in Lynchburg, Virginia. I parked my bike and just had to stop and gaze, taking a long moment to sit on a stone wall that fringed the street side of the property.

Like that first time I hopped atop the train car and beheld the foreign world around me outside of Lynchburg, I sat in wonderment and watched, as people in brightly colored clothes walked by me. I gazed as tiny ocean swells, nudged by a steamy breeze, lapped softly onto the shore. The traffic began to die down and the air cleared of exhaust, allowing me to smell the ocean, flowers, and food aromas from restaurants. My senses became overloaded, filling me with euphoria. I might have sat there for an hour, or maybe longer, as I completely lost track of time.

Of course, all of that thinking, smelling, and seeing can get a guy awfully thirsty. Eventually, I broke from my reverie, pushed my bike into a proper parking spot, and made my way to a Mai Tai bar I had spotted on the second floor of a nearby outside shopping and hotel complex that faced the ocean from across the main street. I ordered their signature drink and it was maybe the best I'd ever tasted. *Nectar of the gods.*

Even more magnificent than the fruity taste of the Mai Tai was the view from the bar—peering onto the crowded sidewalk below and across to the ocean, with shimmering images of the hotels reflecting off it. Given the atmosphere and the fine quality of the drinks, I couldn't stay for just one cocktail, so I ordered a second. And two begat three. And three begat me becoming friends with everyone in the bar. And four begat us all becoming best friends.

I cut myself off from alcohol after the fourth drink and ordered a meal to sober up before getting back on my motorcycle and proceeding onward through the city. Eventually I spotted a couple of dive motels, and I decided, *Time to call it a night. The bus didn't kill me. My stomach is full. I'm feeling good. What a day!*

Inside one of the off-strip waterfront motels, I approached the front desk clerk. The cost was $100 for a night. *I can't afford this forever, but I can afford it tonight,* I thought, and put my payment in cash on the counter. My room was as seedy and disheveled as the guy at the desk, especially compared to the likes of the Hilton, where I had just been lingering for so long, but I didn't mind. Besides, it had a window facing the water, with a breeze blowing through it. Before hitting the sack, I walked onto the beach, my bare feet sinking into the cool sand. *This is it!,* I told myself. *You've done it! Congratulations! Pat yourself on the back!*

This moment was the end of a long-imagined journey

to paradise and equally exciting, a great beginning point of all new unknown adventures and journeys to come.

That night, I slept like the dead. Long past sunrise, I finally awoke to the sound of thunder so loud that I jumped out of bed landing on both feet before I even woke up. The booming sounded like the roof was collapsing on top of me. I looked out my window to see curtains of rain, waving. The carpeted floor beneath the window soaked my feet, telling me the rainstorm had started quite a while earlier. I closed the window. The scene on the other side of the pane would have been beautiful if it were not for the fact that I had to check out of the motel soon, and my only mode of transportation was a motorcycle.

A half-hour passed and there was no letup in the rain. An hour passed, and still the heavy storm didn't slow down. Then after about 90 minutes, the time arrived for me to turn in the room key. The rain was beating down like what Noah saw straight out of the Old Testament. I walked to the front desk and there was a different guy stationed there smoking a thick, half-chewed cigar. He had slick black hair, a week-old stubbly beard, and was wearing a sweaty short-sleeved shirt and a steely scowl that said, "Keep the hell away from me." He looked meaner than a one-eared alley cat.

I approached him gingerly and said, "Hey buddy, that rain sure is coming down. When do you think it'll stop?"

He turned his head up at me and growled. "April."

"What do you mean?"

"Kid, this is monsoon season. It rains all the time now. Won't slow down till April!"

"You're kidding me!" I said, thinking about that brand-new motorcycle I had just bought.

"Nope," he replied, not interested in conversing.

I pictured my motorcycle traversing through nonstop sheets of torrential rain instead of gliding me to places of freedom and delight. "Well, can I get a little more time before I check out? Maybe it'll stop *monsooning* long enough so I can find someplace else to shelter."

I was trying to conserve money and spending another $100 on that place was out of the question.

"Sure, take another hour. You're good till noon. If you're around after that, you gotta pay me for another day," he grumbled.

I turned to go back to my room. The rain kept falling and I knew I had a situation on my hands. This wasn't a storm like anything I had seen in Virginia or Atlanta. These raindrops were like heavy rocks being thrown down from the sky. Paradise wasn't quite as perfect as I thought, but I was set on making the best of it.

When noon arrived, I walked out of the motel and got pelted by the rain. Within 30 seconds, I looked like a drowned cat. I kick-started my bike and drove to the only place in Hawaii where anyone with a friendly face knew my name: the Yamaha dealer. On the way, my visibility was so impaired I couldn't see the vehicles in front of me. Any bike in any rainstorm is dangerous and being out there in this weather was downright foolhardy. Still, I had nowhere else to go.

Somehow the weather gods allowed me to safely reach the dealer, where the service bay doors were open. I drove inside and peeled myself off the bike seat. If you had dropped me one hundred feet underwater, I could not have been more sopping wet than I was right then. A small lake formed at my feet, as I stood in front of the guys in the service department repairing bikes. I was their morning entertainment.

"I got a bike here yesterday . . . " I started, not quite knowing what to say from there.

"Yeah, hey Guy. How's it going?"

The idea formed in my head that I needed to find a way to linger there as long as possible till the weather broke. I said, "Well, I got the bike at closing, and we didn't have a chance to chat it up. I wanted to ask a few questions about it."

"What do you want to know?" one of the guys asked, a smile still plastered across his face at the spectacle of talking to a walking human waterspout.

"Let's start with the tire pressure, and then move on to the engine," I said as I planned on a lengthy point-by-point inspection.

Before my clothes even began to dry, I was hitting it off with the fellas. I asked if the rain truly was gonna fall till April. They said no, the guy was lying. After the inspection was finished, they let me keep hanging out. I didn't interfere with their work, and I was probably a good diversion. When they went to lunch in a car (thank you very much), I joined them, and when they returned to the service bay afterward, I did, too. I had nowhere else to go, and there was still little break in the rain.

During our conversation, they told me the cheapest place to stay was the YMCA. They said it was clean, and the beds were nice. It occupied an old midrise in Honolulu that used to house the Royal Hawaiian Hotel. They said I'd like it.

The storm clouds finally broke around five o'clock that evening, so I said goodbye to my daylong buddies and followed their directions back down Nimitz Highway to the YMCA. They were right about how inviting the place was for a YMCA. It seemed more like a luxury youth hostel. I entered the lobby and spoke to the young fellow behind the desk. He told me they took rates by the night, week, or month. I paid for a month, then rode my bike around back where the YMCA kept a rack and chained it up.

From there, I took the elevator up to my own private room that offered the basics: a spring frame and a mattress, a cheap throw rug on the floor, sink and a closet and most importantly, a window for the sun's rays in the morning. *Home, sweet home, Hawaii!*

After getting situated, I took the elevator back down to the lobby and grabbed a seat at the counter of a cafe next door to the YMCA. I ordered a cheeseburger, some fries, and a Coke. During this downtime, I finally had a few minutes to assess my situation. I had sold nearly all my worldly possessions and left all friends and family behind in Virginia and Atlanta. I didn't have a job. I didn't know what the next day held in store, let alone the next week or month. I had a tantalizing, but vague, notion of traveling the world but no set timetable or concrete destinations in mind. In other words, everything was perfect. At least until the waitress handed me the check. The cost was three times what I'd pay for a cheeseburger and fries back home. *Oh man, I might have accommodations for a month or two, but food is gonna start to be a problem*, I thought. Doing the math, I realized I had enough cash to last me ~sixty days. I created a plan fit for any penniless, yearning wanderer: spend the next month learning my way around the island, then the month after find work. In my tired mind, I thought I'd shine shoes, wait tables, whatever need be that paid for the basics.

CHAPTER XI

# Kissing the Waves of Change

*"There's a whole world out there, right outside
your window. You'd be a fool to miss it."*

—Charlotte Eriksson

THE NEXT MORNING, I woke up with the sun shining in my face, and I felt ready to conquer Oahu. I had nowhere to be but everywhere to go. I hopped on my bike and began to drive down the highway, avoiding the bus lane. Then I did what comes most naturally to me: explore—the sights, sounds, smells, and human experience. I rode down back streets and main thoroughfares. I lingered at scenic over-looks and sped across the sugarcane and pineapple fields.

On the southeastern tip of the island, past the towering cliffs above Makapu'u Beach on the winding Kalanianaole Highway, I discovered a bird sanctuary and aquarium called Sea Life Park. Because I didn't want to spend any money, I simply parked in the lot and watched the people come and go and listened to the sounds of the dolphin and sea lion shows.

Upon getting back on the highway, I passed an oceanic institute and the Kaupo Beach Park—on a sliver of white sand that was once home to an ancient fishing village. There's a rock just offshore called Pohaku Pa'akiki that in Hawaiian mythology is a monument to the agreement between the islanders and a guardian shark that there would be no shark attacks in these waters. I pulled over often to watch the beaches. The sand was so fine, and the emerald water so inviting, I felt like was living in the pages of a travel magazine.

A few miles down the road I discovered an underwater park and pulled over. There was no cost of admission, and several people were out snorkeling. The notion of an underwater park blew me away—but somehow here it made sense. The wildlife just past the shore and underwater was as beautiful as any you'd find in the forests that carpet the island's volcanic mountainsides.

My next discovery was the Hawaiian Village, a tourist trap where they celebrate the heritage of the Pacific Islands by putting on a daily Luau, all-you-can eat buffet and an evening show involving men throwing fire knives and women dancing in grass skirts. The property also has seven mini "villages" representing all the Pacific Island cultures, like Samoa, Tahiti, Tonga, and Fiji. I stepped over the thin, hanging chain rope at the entryway and gave myself a self-guided tour. I didn't stay long because I wanted to keep exploring the island, but the park was a fun diversion and there were so many wonderful cultural activities and exhibits.

After, I passed along the North Shore Coast, seeing the names of every surf spot I knew by heart from watching the Beach-Blanket-Bingo movies and "Endless Summer," like

Sunset Beach, Chun's Reef, Turtle Beach, and Kawela Bay. I turned first into Sunset Beach area and meandered down a dirt road through a banana farm. The fruit wasn't like the kind you see in the grocery store; they were smaller. I ate six of them, and then dropped myself on the beach, looking like a sheep among goats in my blue jeans and sneakers without a bathing suit or towel. From my spot in the sand, I watched the surfers with awe and a healthy dose of envy. I imagined what a thrill it must be to ride a wave, being so balanced and tuned with the powers of nature.

Next, I rode to Waimea Bay, and to my surprise, it was empty. I couldn't believe it—as if the Polynesian gods were giving me a treat. It turns out that the only time Waimea attracts people is during surf competitions. Otherwise, everyone prefers Sunset. From there, the drive back to town was slightly anticlimactic—which makes sense, given that I had just spent the better part of a day admiring the most scenic shoreline in the world. I took the expressway, called the Kamehameha Highway, which slices inland through pineapple plantations and an army air base before turning at Pearl Harbor toward Honolulu. I spent a quiet evening at the YMCA, thinking about the surfers at Sunset Beach, and the idea struck me for my next day's mission: learn to ride a wave. It was settled.

On day three, the sun blasting through the window woke me. I opened my eyes and said, "Okay, the surf's calling you."

I had watched surfers on TV and the big screen my whole life. It didn't look that hard. I knew I'd be able to learn the sport pretty easily. I rode my bike down to Waikiki and discovered I could rent a board for $8 a day. I couldn't believe the price was so cheap. The vendors lining the beach told me that as a beginner I needed to get a longer board, because it was more stable and easier to learn on. After sizing up the scene on the beach for a short while, I walked up to one of the surf stands and said, "Give me your biggest board."

The guy handed me an eight-foot board, and I handed him the cash. I carried it to the water's edge and watched the technique of the skilled surfers, making mental notes of everything they did, and visualizing myself copying them. Then I put my board in the water, about waist-deep, and climbed onto it. My first time on a surfboard—another first!

I paddled out close to a small cluster of tourists on boards surrounding this one godlike, clearly Hawaiian surfer, whose skin was tanned darker than a horse's hide. He was giving group lessons to the Hilton Hawaiian Village guests. I floated just close enough to listen to what was being said. He knew what I was doing but didn't care. After an hour of watching the incredible failure of the tourists he was teaching, I paddled off a distance, and raced into the break surf line of surfers waiting for a wave.

When my turn came, I paddled as hard as I could, felt the momentum of the ocean rising beneath me, and got up—my hands pushing me to my knees, and then lifting me to an awkward standing position. The feeling was glorious, with the tropical breeze massaging my wet skin and the sun warming my shoulders. I caught the wave at just the precise, perfect moment, and I rode it almost the entire way to the sandy shore. It seemed like about 100 yards of surfing, if I had to guess, and I rode what I felt was the full length of a football field. I kissed the waves. It was almost as satisfying as kissing a girl.

The rest of that day, I just surfed, and surfed, and

surfed—till I dropped from exhaustion. If I had died right then and there, heaven would have seemed like a disappointment. When I returned the board to the guy at the surf stand, I said: "What's your name?"

"Jimmy."

"Well Jimmy, I'm Guy, and I'm going to be your best customer. I'll spend $8 every damned day!"

"Sounds good," he said.

"See you tomorrow. Keep that board handy. I'm going to come back to put my damn name on it."

"Okay, see you tomorrow, Guy." Jimmy was pretty deadpan. He had seen enough diehard tourist surfers negotiating the waves.

I was starting to like Hawaii and was brimming with confidence from my flawless day of surfing. I was ready to start exploring and enjoying the nightlife. The question was where to start. I decided to ask the ultimate source in travel wisdom: cab drivers. A bunch of taxis assembled at a stand in front of the YMCA every evening. I walked up to them and asked the best place to get a cheap bite to eat and a cold drink. They introduced me to a row of restaurants and bars downtown that I soon began to visit each night. Over time, I became friendly with a lot of the regulars and got to know them well.

For instance, I met a couple of guys who rode Kawasaki bikes similar to my on and off road Yamaha. I first noticed them as they were parking in front of a bar I'd been frequenting. We got to talking and they told me they were in the Navy, stationed at Pearl Harbor. They worked on submarines. We ended up getting together a lot, whether it was for hitting the bars or going for motorcycle rides. They had been in Hawaii for a while, so they knew of all sorts of great routes on the dirt roads that wound among the dormant volcanoes and plantations that filled the island.

One of the finest contributions these Navy guys made to my off-road motorcycle skills and adventuring was their love of riding in these boundless, open areas of rugged landscape in the rain. I'm not talking about rain as you may think about rain. I'm talking about the dreaded monsoons where you honestly believe the sky is falling.

It takes a while to get used to the feeling that each and every drowned cat feels. There is wet, and then there is wet to the bone. A favorite game of chase was each following the other in various sequences, where everybody would get a chance to plow into standing water on the ground and gun the back wheel of the motorcycle, creating a mud rooster tail of ten to fifteen feet straight up in the air.

Then, there was that special day where it was my turn to show the Navy boys how the Virginia boys do it. I picked out a particularly large puddle of water, took the lead position, and designed my best rooster tail on planet earth to come. Next, I found out my most desirable-looking puddle was a massive water-filled eight-foot hole in the ground. As I accelerated my bike to the highest and optimum speed of approach, it surface-glided for a full two seconds before it sank into the eight-foot hole.

Naturally, I did not surrender my death grips on the handlebars and sunk to the realization that comes when you meet that moment to decide: you must either sink or swim. Clearly, because I'm still here, I decided the latter. However, that's where the fun stopped. The dry weight of my motorcycle was approximately 130 pounds. Now wet and underwater, God only knew.

Kneeing my way back to surface earth, my Navy friends

were falling off their parked motorcycles with uproarious laughter. It may not be obvious to all, but it's most difficult to fume in monsoonal rain, so within a minute or two, I joined the laughter.

Then came the moment of decision whether to leave the motorcycle to come back some day after the rain and floods, or not. I chose not to. What took place next was my breaking a heretofore human record of breath control as my friends each held one of my legs as I went upside-down into this small lake to fold my arms around the frame and have them pull me, and pivot the bike, out of water high enough that a handlebar was barely able to be seen above the water. Pushing the handlebar into the soft mud to give it a moment of stay and the ability of surface reach, I then surfaced to breathe after what seemed to be a lifetime of not breathing.

It took more than an hour, but my bike was retrieved, kickstand back on the ground. It looked fine after its nice bath, but I looked like some kind of mud monster out of a low budget B-movie. Then the only question remained: *Would it start?* I looked to my friends for advice, and nobody had a clue what to expect. So, then the moment came for that decision. I mounted my bike, gave the kickstart the kick of its life, and it turned on. Needless to say, next stop was the closest bar and 14 rolls of paper towels.

These Navy guys and I became inseparable and had many such extraordinary adventures riding up rockfaces and near straight-drop falls off the volcanic, mountainous terrains over and over again. Seldom was it the same path.

One night, they offered to take me onto the Navy base to give me a tour of their nuclear submarine. We rode our bikes to the front gate, and one of their buddies let us in. I followed them on my motorcycle from there until I suddenly—and painfully—learned a fun fact about Pearl Harbor: the railroad rails along the piers there are sunken into the pavement, and they're almost invisible in the dusk/dark. My front tire got nestled into the wide impression that housed one of the rails, and I got thrown hind-over-teakettle onto my back at the concrete edge of a pier that housed giant Navy ships. My helmet *thunked* off the pavement and I was left dazed and confused for a few moments. After collecting my senses, I looked around and realized that if I had traveled in the air a few feet more, I would have been thrown over the docking pier and plummeted about 50 feet into the water.

If I had survived the fall and didn't drown in the nasty petroleum-filled muck, I would have had to tread water for at least an hour before someone could have found a way to pull me up to safety. I slowly stood as my buddies surrounded me. Fortunately, I was just scratched up and shaken, but okay. Still bound and determined to complete our mission, we continued onward to the submarine, where I got the most amazing tour.

If I had tried to sneak on board, I probably would have been shot. But I was with friends, who talked my way past their (buddies') guards at the gangplank and took me through every corner of the vessel. It was yet another first for me: my first time on a nuclear sub. Another door had opened in my life's adventures. Once again, I walked through with eagerness. What surprised me most about the tour was how small the submarine was. I expected something bigger. It sure wouldn't be mistaken for a cruise ship.

Soon thereafter, I met Jay and Glenn, who became my non-bike riding closest buddies on the island and played an important role in my yet unknown stowaway adventure aboard a cruise ship on its round-the-world trip. The two of them were both staying at the YMCA at the same time I was—until the three of us moved to the bordello, of course . . . .

I was introduced to Glenn first. He and I were sitting next to each other on a worn-out red leather couch in the outdoor patio TV lounge at the YMCA, and he was smoking a joint, high as the Hindenburg, taking drags on it like he was inhaling his last precious breaths on Earth.

Glenn turned to me. "You want some?"

"Sure," I said, taking the joint from him. We talked for hours after that—or maybe it was minutes, as I lost my sense of time and place pretty fast. Regardless, we became good friends as we got stoned together and discussed our common-sense answers for all the world's most pressing problems. The next night, he introduced me to his good friend, Jay.

If you've ever seen the movie "Oliver," picture, for a moment, Jay as Fagin, and Glenn as the Artful Dodger. Glenn was scrappy, a bit more impressionable and not nearly as worldly. He was the sidekick to Jay, who was a mid-40s, charismatic, conniving, brilliant, street savvy, charming-when-he-wanted-to-be fellow—who happened to be hiding a dark past. They were quite a pair, and I still think of them fondly. If I had to assign myself a character in this threesome, I'd say I was Oliver Twist. They taught me the ways of the world they inhabited, of living large on pennies a day in Honolulu by playing all sorts of angles— but at the same time, I always remained slightly an outsider.

Jay was on the lam from the federal government. He was a forged-papered medical doctor who ran a pill mill for the mob in San Francisco. He enjoyed about a two-year run with this gig and made a ton of money for everybody involved until the DEA busted him and threw him in jail. The mob paid his bail, bought him a one-way ticket to Honolulu and told him they'd bring him back to California when the heat cooled down. I knew less about Glenn. He was maybe about 30 years old and from the Pacific Northwest. Jay had also enjoyed a short career as a Hollywood stuntman, which made for an interesting conversation starter at bars and knew all sorts of things about pyrotechnics. Glenn, I thought, just skipped the rat race to come to Hawaii to enjoy endless sex and drugs.

The three of us became a trio—inseparable—having fun on the town and exploring the island until the end of the second month, when my money ran out. Every so often, Glenn earned cash by washing school buses. It was enough to pay for a night full of drinking and food, and to keep a roof over himself at the Y. I'm not sure exactly how Jay got his money, but he never had much of it either.

I decided to start applying for accounting positions, so I could enjoy a more sustainable life on the island for another year or two, as I had planned all along. To this end, I cut my hair nice and neat, so I'd look more like a business like than a hippie surfer (which I felt like from within). I put on my khaki pants and a clean, pressed shirt and began knocking on doors at the administrative offices of the big hotels in Honolulu. At each stop, I handed the manager or human resources person a freshly printed copy of my quite long and impressive resume. I'd say something like, "I'd like to be a night auditor in the accounting office."

Every time, I received the same reply: "We don't have anything open right now, but we'll keep your resume on file."

After a couple of days of door-knocking, I described the experience to a girl at a bar. "I don't know if I'm putting somebody off, or what's happening."

"You don't understand," she told me. "The reason nobody's hiring you is because you're a haole."

"I beg your pardon?"

"A *haole*. An outsider. To Hawaiian natives, haoles only come over here to party and overdose on drugs. This is a tight-knit community and they're never gonna let you in."

"You're kidding me!" I said, but deep down, her words rung true.

Given my experience and skills, I should have seemed like a dream gift to the accounting departments of those hotels, one dropped into their offices by the gods. Instead, I pretty much saw them eyeing the trash can as I handed them my resume. *A haole.* Suddenly, my two-year plan started to look like it might need revising. I didn't mind doing whatever work was necessary to pay the bills, but only for the short term. If I planned to live anywhere for an extended period, I wanted to put my accounting skills to work.

At the same time, my current lodgings were about to expire, so I went looking for cheaper alternatives. Some friends gave me leads, but each one turned into a dead end. Finally, I found a dark, dank terrace apartment that an old Asian woman was willing to rent to me. The monthly cost was about half of what the YMCA charged. It was a complete dump. If all you did was hang out there all day, you'd eventually want to kill yourself. Even the cockroaches hated it!

The woman told me, "You not find other place. I tell you. You can have this. You not find other place."

"Why?" I asked.

"Because you're a haole. I'll rent because I'm nice. We've had three haoles in here, and all three of them died of overdoses."

No matter how charming her invitation was, I respectfully declined. After that, Jay, Glenn, and I pooled our resources together and shared one room at the Y.

Now that it was made clear that working in my chosen profession was not an option, it was incumbent upon me to make the best of it. There was nothing more to do than to enjoy the island's kaleidoscope of hospitalities.

CHAPTER XII

# *Island Hospitalities*

*"I do not want to get to the end of my life and
find that I just lived the length of it. I want
to have lived the width of it as well."*

—*Diane Ackerman*

**THE NEW ROOM** had one of the larger windows in it. In my luck-of-the-draw, I slept where when the minute the sun rose out of the ocean, it would hit my closed eyelids like a laser beam. Try as I would, there was not much sleep after sunrise. One fine day, I woke up with bristled tail committed to find the end of the rainbow. It had been a notion that occurred to me more than once as I drove past Oahu's vibrant rainforest on the northeastern side of the island. Typically, around lunch time each day, the rainforest would produce the most grandiose, brightest rainbow that could be seen for 10 miles when traveling up the northeastern highway side of the island.

Today was the day that, no-holes-barred, I, on the wings of my motorcycle, would travel to that legendary spot: the end

107

of the rainbow. At lunch, I took out towards the northeastern highway. In about fifteen minutes, I spotted a rainbow! Now it was a matter of navigating without borders, boundaries, or fencing to arrive at its end. Armed as I was since a child, I had my trusty rusty wire cutters in my back pocket. I wound through neighborhood after neighborhood, through open fields, through somebody's backyard with a pool (that didn't much care for it), to arrive at a very particular non-entrance to the rainforest. The rainforest has a nicely developed road system for tourists and residents to come in and out to enjoy their rainforest. Unfortunately, the rainbow cared not for civil engineering. As I entered the rainforest, it was in full rainforest regalia. Due to the density of being a rainforest, alas, my motorcycle could travel no further. Feverishly on foot, I knew that time was of the essence. Weaving and dodging the plant life, I arrived at the end of the rainbow.

Rainbows, as you may or not have thought about, are nothing but dangling water beads being struck by the sun. With my head placed completely under the beginning or end (depending on your vantage point), the air that my lungs inhaled was like no air I had ever breathed before. The water droplets were flavored with a sweetness and aroma that is simply indescribable. I stood there in a world of no sound staring and breathing deeply in reverence until the rainbow was no more.

There are sometimes in your life where second place is not so bad. I say this because clearly today, I was the second fortunate soul to arrive at the end of this rainbow; the pot of gold had apparently been taken by the first.

And then there was the day we were all awakened by the loud knocking on our door. A couple of the YMCA buddies had discovered a jewel in the mist. Namely, the Primo Beer factory. Never thought about it; never knew . . . but as it turned out, the most proud and prestigious beer brewed in the islands at that time was Primo Beer.

I had partaken in Primo Beer often without ever bringing to wonder where it came from. It was just good, not expensive, and was a local crowd favorite. The door knock friends, who had just discovered the day before that the Primo Beer factory on Nimitz Highway offered free factory tours and tastings, said they were ready to go again. After the tour, the attendees could sit on the beautiful blue water green grass shore of Pearl Harbor on picnic tables filled with baskets and baskets of fabulous, extra salty pretzels . . . and all the Primo Beer you could drink.

Once that was made clear, all flags flew towards the Primo Factory that day. Being the only one with transportation, I joined the six-man gang piling onto one of the Honolulu metropolitan buses. We arrived a few minutes before the 1:00 p.m. Wednesday tour and made up the majority of the tour line. Fascinating wasn't the word. In retrospect, the only word I would call it would be *intoxicating*.

As billed in our buddy's description, the tour ended in a perfectly beautiful, scenic, large grass sitting area with the waves of Pearl Harbor's waters gently caressing the shore. In the background, they played traditional island music, some of which I recognized from one of Elvis Presley's Hawaiian movies. *Grin, grin.* Again, as billed, the picnic tables (which could hold four on each side, eight to a table) had three large baskets of the best salted pretzels I've ever experienced.

I'm sure you could guess where the rest of this story is going. However, I'll be pleased to confirm your suspicions. One pitcher begot two, two begot three. I won't belabor the point, but sometime after the twentieth pitcher, no one at the table could stand with such a degree of acumen to retrieve any further bowl of pretzels. The only reason I believe we weren't asked to leave before closing time was the sincerity of our laughter. Other tour attendees would come and go from the picnic grounds after the 2:00, 3:00, and 4:00 p.m. tours, but wouldn't stay for any length of time (my guess is that those guests had a better time because *we* were having a *great* time). Then, as all good things come to an end, the 4:00 p.m. tour attendees that came out of the factory at 5:00 p.m. and were notified that there was only 30 minutes left before the gardens were closed.

As I mentioned, our crew came on a bus. This, all by itself, was another first for me. Riding a bus in Honolulu wasn't ever necessary due to my motorcycle. Whether it was forgetfulness or oblivion, the ramifications of riding home on the bus weren't fully appreciated until we all helped one another to successfully climb the mountainous three steps required from the bus stop curb to enter the main body of the bus.

It was rush hour. Who knew? We didn't. What happened next may still be talked about in the annals of bus drivers' history in the Hawaiian union locker rooms to this day. The bus driver pressed down on the accelerator pedal at a speed to assure his place in rush hour traffic. There being no seats, our only salvation was the hang-down handles from the roof to maintain only the representation of our upright posture. The force of the momentum, caused by the reckless act of the bus driver's acceleration, in turn, caused each and every one of our crew's bodies to be flung like bowling balls through the crowd sitting and standing until our limp bodies came to rest at the back of the bus. To hear the wails of the maddening passengers, they almost certainly dwarfed the legendary, high-pitched sounds of Ulysses' fabled "Sirens." The bus driver, now only about fifty yards from his point of departure, slammed on the breaks and back we all came to the front of the bus. This wasn't exactly the "round trip" we had imagined when we took off earlier in the day. The bus driver promptly pressed the button to open the gas-pressured doors and by collar and belt, threw each of us out (fortunately) onto a grass field. There's no way to know what happened after we left the commuters on the bus, but it's safe to say, that we were all safer no longer being a part of that bus ride.

It was getting to be dark, or our eyes couldn't refract much light, so we all laid on the ground where we were cast and promptly fell asleep. I don't remember which one of us woke up first, but it was way late in the night. So late that the buses had stopped running. We were on our own to walk all the way back to the Y. The 10-mile or so hike ended a little after 2:00 in the morning, and that very next day, we were all able to confirm that, yes, Primo Beer did give free samples of its product to all that would attend their tour. However, none of us were thirsty for beer, Primo or otherwise, for some time to come.

The next day, little did I know, Jay met Harry, and everything really changed from there. I mean, everything.

Harry was a native Hawaiian who ran a spiffy little bordello on the second floor of a building on King Street in Chinatown, and he loved to play poker. All. The. Time. If Harry was awake, he was either eating, attending to his girls' needs, or playing poker. Or doing all three. He always wore a pair of sandals, shorts, and a different flowery Hawaiian shirt every day.

When you walked up the stairs into his establishment, the first thing you saw was the split wooden door—with the top wide open, and wide tray bottom closed—that led into his office. Inside it, he kept a La-Z-Boy reclining chair and a poker table with seats arranged around it. There was always a game going, and Jay had somehow gotten in on them. The pots were usually small because Harry wasn't so interested in the money as in the game itself.

Jay introduced me and Glenn to him and we all joined in the fun. Whenever we lost to Harry, he was never concerned about the cash. Harry let us play for IOUs until we eventually won our money back. The whole time we sat at the table, he would feed us Chinese takeout. We could order whatever we wanted. He was tremendously generous—and he could afford to be. His bordello had thirteen rooms, and girls were working in them in shifts practically twenty-four hours a day, seven days a week. His main clients were the Navy boys from Pearl Harbor.

During our games, girls would enter the office and hand Harry a purse full of cash. He'd count it by simply weighing it in his hand, then throw it in a drawer in his desk. Everybody knew exactly where he kept his money, just as they knew if they tried to touch it, they would be kissing off their last day on earth. By this point, Jay, Glenn, and I were down to our last nubs of cash. We didn't have enough to pay for another month of rent anywhere, so we settled on a plan to start sleeping in the lifeguard stands at a nearby beach. By scoping out the scene we saw that the lifeguards finished work for the day about an hour before dusk and returned the next morning about an hour before dawn. If we set up camp during those in-between hours, no one would be the wiser. *Voila!* Free ocean front sleeping arrangements!

In the evening leading up to our first planned night sleeping in the lifeguard stands, we played poker at Harry's. Nothing happened out of the usual until about 12:30 a.m. when a loud BANG ricocheted off the walls of the bordello. The sound made us jump out of our chairs, and in our beer-soaked stupor, we stumbled out of the office doorway, bouncing into each other like the Three Stooges. When we eventually gathered senses, we realized that Harry had already vanished from the room long before us—without even opening the bottom half of the door. As for the source of the sound: there was no doubt that it was a gunshot.

As soon as the three of us managed to get out of the office, we turned right down the long hallway that led to the ladies' rooms, and saw a sailor jump out an open window at the far end, then climb down the fire escape as his white uniform's back flap waved behind him.

Next, we heard Harry's voice booming from one of the rooms. "Goddamnit! Goddamnit! Goddamnit!"

We entered the room and saw him standing over a bed where one of the girls lay, shot dead. It was tremendously tragic and unthinkable. The three of us were stunned—even Jay, who was once a faux medical professional. I'd never seen a corpse before, another first that I'd been happier to wait on. A crowd of girls formed around us as their Johns quickly dressed and split the scene. Harry, who was as generous to the local law enforcement officers as he was to everyone else, called the police.

He came back to the room and stood next to the bed. "Goddamnit, I hate when this happens," he said. *When this happens?* I thought. *When this happens?* I clearly wasn't in Lynchburg, Virginia anymore.

A few minutes later, about seven or eight cops arrived

and exchanged pleasantries with Harry. Most were customers of his and all adored him. Several knew the victim. The scene turned into a strange social event. I couldn't believe it.

"Betty Sue was a good girl," Harry told the officers. "I don't know why this had to happen. What a waste! She was one of my favorites."

One of the officers said, "Harry, we're so sorry. What did the guy look like?"

"He looked like the rest of them. A sailor."

A cop asked us what we saw, but we didn't have much in the way of helpful information either. He didn't press us. I learned during my time in Hawaii that the police there were the most casual police officers in the world. Unless you unzipped your fly in front of them and peed on their leg, they weren't going to bother you. The police department in Honolulu didn't even have a fleet of patrol cars. The officers were given stipends and they bought their own vehicles—most bought an Oldsmobile Cutlass Sierra. I think only one sedan with flashing lights was parked outside of Harry's building on that night.

After the coroner rolled away the body, the police left, and the entire bordello seemed to exhale. We all knew, sadly, that no one would try to find the sailor. As much as I loved "Hawaii Five-O" on TV, the reality was much different. Steve McGarrett and Danno would not be booking anyone in this episode. I looked at my watch and it said, 2:00 a.m. Harry suggested we play some more cards to settle down. My friends and I agreed. He treated us to another round of Chinese takeout for our troubles.

By 4:00 a.m., none of us could keep our eyes open. The notion of wandering out to the lifeguard stands to catch maybe ninety minutes of sleep before the lifeguards arrived seemed about as inviting as squeezing lemon on a sunburn. That's when Jay came up with his idea. His brilliant, callous, practical idea. He looked up at Harry as we were cleaning up the table and said, "Now that you've got an empty room, you mind if we crash in it for the night?"

"Don't you have anyplace else to stay?" he asked.

"Actually, we don't. We're not staying at the Y anymore and we're out of money besides what we're winning from you. We'll just sleep in the room until you replace Betty Sue. What do you say?"

Harry paused for a moment and said, "Sure. That's fine. The room is yours."

Jay, Glenn, and I stumbled down the hallway and into the now vacant room. Glenn and I retrieved a new mattress out of one of Harry's locked rooms and we were back in the 'dry when it rains' business. Then Jay announced, "Look, as much as I love you guys, there's only going to be two of us on this bed. One of us has to be on the floor."

Glenn and I nodded. Jay continued. "We can rotate each night. This is a good gig. Harry likes us and will probably let us keep it going for a while. Now, let's flip a coin to see who's on the bed."

Jay pulled out a coin and let me call a side first. I chose "heads" and won.

Glenn then chose "tails." He won, too. Jay refused to sleep on the floor. "Well damn it all, it's my quarter," he growled.

Glenn and I equally refused to give in, and eventually, Jay surrendered and settled on the wooden floor. I didn't realize as I finally nodded off to sleep, just before sunrise, that this restful respite was to be short lived. No more than two hours later, Glenn and I awakened to the sight and sound of Jay screaming at the top of his lungs jumping up and down on the wooden floor, never landing on either of his two feet on the ground at the same time. Turns out Jay picked up a bug traveler inside his right ear.

Jay was hitting the opposite side of his head, feverishly trying to knock it out. It is a sight and sound that I'll never forget. Jenny, the sweetheart of the girl next door, came roaring into our room, "What the fuck is going on here? Us working girls need our sleep as well." Glenn and I approached Jay trying to figure out a way to help. But it was Jenny that quickly took charge. She jerked Jay over to the bed and pushed him plenty hard to fall flat. She then sat next to him and forced his head onto her lap. She inserted her index finger and thumb into the violated ear like tweezers and with all the grace of a Bavarian conductor, thrusted her arm outward in a waving motion, loudly declaring "I've got it, now calm the fuck down." Jenny stood up and marched out to her room next door turning, smiling, and winking at Glenn and me.

God knows, and I don't know, if she physically extracted the menacing insect but thankfully Jay accepted it as so. After he somewhat rebooted his demeanor, Jay declared his turn for sleeping on the floor was DONE. At twenty-one years old, it's easy to say sleep is completely overrated so I gave up my side of the bed and Jay and Glenn finished their sleep. I went over to Jenny's room and found comfort. A few days later, another milestone moment arrived (quite literally) and it came to mark the beginning of the end to my short, sweet happy life in Hawaii.

# CHAPTER XIII

# Seduced by the SS Canberra

*"Then one day, when you least expect it,
the great adventure finds you."*

—*Ewan McGregor*

**DESPITE THE EARLY** hour, the sun was already burning, and I felt the need to get out and enjoy it, so I walked out of the room and down the stairway onto the well populated Chinatown sidewalk. Hours later, after a great visit with some friends still living at the Y, I returned, refreshed, to find Harry, Jay and Glenn playing poker in the office, and the girls hard at work as sailors filed in and out of Harry's establishment. My Y buddies greeted me like I'd been gone for a month when they saw me. Everything seemed the same as before—with one exception: Jay, Glenn and I were now residents of Honolulu's finest bordello.

It may surprise you to learn that a man truly cannot live in a bordello forever. But while he's there, he sure as hell can have a good time. Especially if he's a twenty-one-year-old Virginia boy with an endless appetite for fun, adventure, and women. I was as happy as Jed Clampett's hound dog sunning out at the cement pond for the time that I called Harry's bordello my home.

Yet, still, I was restless.

My days consisted of playing poker with Harry and the boys, walking over to the nearest bar with my small or large winnings and coming back and sometimes getting to know one of the girls a little better (at no charge, if they weren't busy). Then I'd play some more poker.

Although having one less room available meant reduced revenue for Harry, he didn't seem to mind us crashing at his place every night. He liked the company, and we enjoyed the arrangement. For about a month, the world for me, Jay, and Glenn barely extended beyond a three or four-block radius of Chinatown.

Then one morning, I discovered the most life changing, awe-inspiring, captivating, magnificently beautiful thing I had ever seen: The SS Canberra, a luxury British cruise ship liner. It was a moment that was destined to change my life forever. Just as I was drawn to hopping atop those train cars as a boy in Lynchburg, which led me into the Great Unknown World Beyond, I instantly saw this ship's potential as my next ultimate vehicle for exploration and discovery. I absolutely had to learn more.

I first laid eyes upon it as Jay and I were walking down the stairs from Harry's place to grab breakfast at one of those noodle shacks that sold containers of rice and mystery meat for fifty cents. Chinatown lies northwest of downtown Honolulu, on the edge of a bay along a network of pro-tected deep-water piers and docks. Occasionally, we'd hear the low sound of a rusty container ship's horn announcing its approach to the docks, but I never really paid the boats or ship traffic much attention.

On this particular morning, though, I couldn't help but notice the massive hull of a ship literally blocking out the sun as I stepped onto the sidewalk with Jay. It towered above the one-story storefronts across the street from us, casting its massive shadow like a mountain. The Canberra was docked next to the 10-story Aloha Tower Terminal, and rose almost as high as it, turning Honolulu's giant land-mark into a sewing needle by comparison. I had never seen a cruise ship before.

"Jay, that's got to be the biggest object on the planet!" I exclaimed. "What in the hell is that?"

"Well, obviously it's a ship," he said.

"I've got to see that thing!"

"Well, what about breakfast?" Jay asked.

"No, no. You go ahead. I'm fine. I'm going to see the ship."

"I'll go with you, then," he said.

The two of us walked to the Aloha ship terminal to behold the SS Canberra, the world's largest luxury liner at that time, measuring a quarter of a mile long and 100 feet high. A couple of gangplanks stretched from the upper terminal floor up to the deck midway up the vessel—one at the bow and another at the stern—and passengers were actively disembarking. The Canberra was like a floating city containing thousands of people, and the terminal was alive with activity. I gaped at the scene, not able to process the information as fast as it passed from my eyes to my brain. After a few minutes, I stopped one of the passengers—an older man.

"Hey, what is this ship?"

"Why, this is the SS Canberra," he replied, in a proper British accent that sounded straight out of public television. "It's on its round-the-world cruise. We left from Southampton, England and we're going back to Southampton, England. It takes about three months. The cruise is simply marvelous."

"Well, thank you very much," I said.

"Cheers," he replied and went on his way.

A cruise ship, traveling around the world for three months. *Eureka!* I turned to Jay and announced, "I'm going with this thing. I'm gone. I'm just g-o-n-e, gone. I am getting aboard this ship. I don't care how, and I don't care when, but when it leaves, I'll be on it."

Jay asked why I'd ever want to leave our current situation at Harry's.

"Well, I've done Hawaii," I said. "I've done everything I want to do. I've seen the place. At the end of the day, this island is just a rock. I need to move on."

I had struck up enough conversations with enough guys at the bars whose stories in Hawaii began similar to mine. They arrived in their early 20s for a good time and to get a taste of surfing and paradise, and a decade later, they were still on the island, never able to scrape up enough money to get an airplane ticket off—and with no prospects once they left. With each year that passed for them, Oahu became smaller and smaller. For many, it long since stopped being a fantasy getaway and turned into little more than a pretty rock. I wasn't going to be stuck on a rock. I was on my way around the world, and I had just found my ride.

Jay was getting a little bored of me standing like a deer in headlights, gawking at the ship, so finally he said, "Are you going to stay here all day?"

"You go on to breakfast without me," I said.

I knew at that moment that my adventures with Fagin and the Artful Dodger had come to their natural end. I was no longer Oliver Twist and was once again Guy, in charge of my life, and following no one's lead. I knew exactly what the next step in my adventures would be. Jay left, and I stood leaning against a wall for another hour or so, watching the ship, assessing the safest, fastest, and easiest way to get on board. I felt just like that kid in Lynchburg, squatting on the embankment near the railroad trestle, measuring how to jump onto a boxcar.

Eventually, I approached the last two elderly women departing the ship who were walking slowly by me. My eyes had followed their path off the Canberra. First, they had stepped onto the gangplank and presented some kind of identification to a ship's Officer. Then, they crossed onto the terminal floor and were met by two serious looking immigration officers at a one-man podium who inspected their boarding passes and passports. The whole time I was enjoying the scene. This was all theater to me. All the while, however, the orderly accountant's side of my brain was making calculations, determining odds, processing the procedures and functions.

I greeted the two women casually. "Good morning, ladies."

"Good morning, young man. We would like to see Pearl Harbor. Do you know how we can get the right bus to it?"

"Absolutely, it would be my pleasure to escort you."

I walked them two blocks to the nearest bus stop and along the way said, "You know, I just think that ship is the most marvelous thing ever. I need to find a way to get on that boat and work my way around the world."

One of the women said, "I heard that someone got on the boat in San Francisco last year, and yes, I do believe they were able to work. They took the ship all the way around the world, I believe." That was all I needed to hear.

When the bus arrived, I helped the women on it. I told the driver, "They want to get off at the Arizona Memorial at Pearl Harbor. Please see that these sweet, little, old ladies make it safely."

"Yeah, sure. Okay."

The bus doors closed as a new set of doors in my life opened, welcoming me to walk through them and onto the SS Canberra.

I didn't walk back to Harry's from the cruise ship terminal, I floated. I had completely forgotten all about breakfast and didn't care. My nourishment came from the anticipation of my upcoming trip. I walked up the stairs to Harry's and down the hall to my room and found Jay, lying on the bed and grinning like the cat who just swallowed the canary.

"Well, what did you discover?" he asked.

I said, "I discovered that I'm going to be sailing around the world soon."

"What if I told you that I could guarantee that I could get you on that ship?"

"You can guarantee all you like because I already know I'm getting on that ship."

"No, no, no, no," he said. "I can absolutely one hundred percent guarantee that you can get on that ship."

"Okay, how can you one hundred percent guarantee me?"

"Before I tell you, I want you to make me a promise. If I can get you on that ship, you have to give me your motorcycle. You're not going to need it and you can't take it with you. That's my price."

"Fine," I replied. "You're absolutely right. I'm not going to need it. If you can absolutely unequivocally guarantee that you'll get me on that ship, then yeah, you can have the motorcycle once I'm on board."

"Shake on it?" he asked, extending his hand.

"Sure, shake." I squeezed firmly. Then I asked him to explain his surefire guaranteed foolproof plan—and it turned out to be maybe the most insane idea I had ever heard. Yet it seemed doable.

I had told him that the ship was scheduled to leave that night at midnight. He said, "Around eleven o'clock, about an hour beforehand, I'm going to strip naked, pour lighter fluid all over my body, light myself on fire, and go running and screaming at the top of my lungs up and down between both gangplanks. I guarantee you, nobody is going to be watching what you do. You can stroll onboard like you're taking a walk down Main Street!"

Lighting yourself on fire might seem like an extreme way to get a free Yamaha motorcycle, but I knew that he was once a stuntman. He insisted he could put on a big, flashy show without actually getting hurt.

I considered his proposal for a few seconds and said, "Done deal! I'm in!"

Suddenly, I realized I needed to tell Glenn about my plan. He had been spending less and less time sleeping at Harry's lately, and more time at the YMCA, where he had been shacking up with a new girl. I ran over there and found him.

"Glenn, listen buddy, I'm leaving." I told him.

Stunned, he said, "Where you going?"

We grabbed lunch together and as we ate, I described everything: seeing the Canberra for the first time, finding out about its round-the-world trip, discovering that I can most likely earn my keep on the ship by working on it, and my plan to get onboard involving Jay getting naked and lighting himself on fire. Afterward, I left Glenn with his girlfriend at the YMCA, and he promised to meet back up with me in the evening before my departure.

When I returned to Harry's the girls mobbed me at the door. Jay had told them I was leaving. They were all excited for me. They treated me like family—giving me hugs, telling me how happy they were, like I had just won the lottery. Harry walked up to me and patted me on the back. "I wish I could go with you," he said, "but you know I can't leave this place."

The reception was fabulous. A couple of the girls told me they wanted to take me to dinner later and I agreed. Then I made the necessary preparations for a last-minute decision to travel around the world by stowing away aboard a cruise ship—which pretty much involved getting rid of my few remaining possessions except for the clothes I was wearing, and my wallet.

In the evening, I showed up at the Chinese restaurant where the girls told me to meet for dinner, and they surprised me with a true *Bon Voyage!* party. They had gotten the word out and about 50 well-wishers showed up. It seemed like every person I had ever befriended or shared a drink with was there, wishing me a good send-off, toasting to my success. I was a celebrity. Everyone there even pitched in and paid for my $19.99 egg roll meal.

"Tonight, we spare no expense for you, Guy!" they said, for my last supper.

As excited as they were for me, they seemed even more excited to watch Jay set himself on fire. They all set their watches. No one wanted to miss the 11 o'clock light show. The crowd eventually filtered out, with about two hours to spare before my departure. The only two who remained were me and Glenn.

"Let's walk over to the ship together, and check things out," I said.

"Okay, I'd love to."

We walked slowly, chatting about nothing, really. I felt badly for Glenn. He had no way off the island. If he went back to Oregon, the likely scenario was that the authorities would get him on the drug bust that he had skipped out on.

We arrived at the ship terminal and took the escalator up to the passenger loading area in the humid, dimly lit rise of forever disappearing steps. I peered at the now better lit terminal passenger loading floor and immediately locked eyes on the gangplanks. The setup was different from the morning. The immigration stand was manned by two night-shift officers who—frankly—looked like they were just a few clowns short of a circus, and there was no longer anyone from the ship standing at the top of the gangplank looking at identification or inspecting tickets. The ship side gang-plank was unattended!

I observed for a few minutes and saw that the embarking passengers would show their passports and boarding passes to the two immigration officers—one fat, one skinny, like Laurel and Hardy—then walk up the gangplank to the ship. *Oh my God, this is going to be easier than I ever possibly imagined!* I didn't know how long it would take for me to find my opening to scoot past the immigration officers, but I knew it would arrive. I just had to be ready for the moment. After about 20 minutes, two portly women strolled up to the stand, carrying all sorts of shopping bags. As one of them reached for her paperwork, one of her bag's straps broke and the contents burst open. She bent down for it, and then her pocketbook fell, its contents emptying on the ground as well. Laurel and Hardy bent over with their backs to me to help her and I looked at Glenn. He stared back at me, wide-eyed. This was my moment.

*Boom!* I scurried past the immigration stand and up the gangplank faster than a scalded dog makes tracks. I tried to look casual as I did it. In a few short seconds, I was on the promenade deck of the ship and Laurel and Hardy were none the wiser.

Standing at the railing, I looked back at Glenn. He was hoppingly excited, waving. I waved back, then turned around, surveying the scene. There was a bank of interior elevators nearby, so I went in and pressed the button. The doors slid open and there was a guy inside pushing the buttons. "Where are you going, sir?" he asked.

*Around the world*, I thought, but after looking at the choices above the elevator's interior door, I said, "To the sun deck, please."

Next thing I knew, I was on the sun deck, which was the highest level of the ship. I walked to the railing and waved excitedly down to Glenn. He spotted me and gave me a thumbs-up, looking as happy as a lark. Suddenly, I remembered Jay's plan to get naked and light himself on fire.

Glenn must have made the same realization at the same time and took off like a bullet. Jay's idea was that if the police or immigration got too close to him, he'd jump into the water to douse himself off and swim away. The piers weren't as tall or fenced off as the ones at Pearl Harbor, so he would have been able to escape safely. After Glenn vanished, this incredible feeling of relief washed over me. I had once again taken the opportunity that life had presented me, and I felt as tall as the Empire State Building. I was headed around the world on a luxury cruise liner.

To calm myself, I plopped onto one of the chaise lounges on the sun deck and took deep breaths. People were milling about, and beside me sat an elderly couple, as casual as can be. The husband was reading a book. It had a title that I didn't recognize, but I noticed that it had a bookmark buried in it and that it had the ship's seal on it, and the seal print read "Canberra Library."

Interesting! I lifted myself from the chaise lounge and walked to an interior entrance where I found a map of the ship. Examining closely, I spotted the library, which was back on the promenade deck. I took the elevator down and walked into it. The library was empty of people, not even a librarian, and was decorated with magnificently comfortable leather sofas and chairs lit by regal-looking crystal lamps.

On the walls, mahogany shelves were stuffed with books. All of them were available for the passengers to borrow on the honor system. I browsed the titles for a few minutes until I found the quintessential one to firmly establish myself as a thoughtful, stately, and well-read resident aboard the USS Canberra for a long trip: *War and Peace*. I pulled it off the shelf and tucked it under my arm. It was the thickest book in the entire library. With it, I would assume the role of a passenger—with no luggage, cabin, or worldly goods, and only $15 to my name.

*Next stop, Southampton England, baby!* I thought. About this time, the ship air horns signaled that it was time to depart, so I ran to the rail and looked onto the terminal deck. Nearly everyone who celebrated my last supper was there, including Jay. He spotted me and started grinning ear-to-ear. I shook my head at him to say, "No, that motorcycle's not yours. You didn't get me on this ship!"

He simply shook his head back again smiling ear to ear, mouthing, "I've got your bike, and there's absolutely nothing you can do about it!"

Jay was the happiest guy on the deck. He had a new motorcycle and didn't even need to get naked or light himself on fire for it. I didn't let it get me down though. The moment was too thrilling. I was living my dream of going around the world.

Quite unexpectedly on the dot of 11:45 p.m., a marching band began parading onto the terminal deck drumming as they marched in place and then once in place struck up a rousing melody of familiar show tunes and current hits. The ship's staff handed out streamers and noise makers to all the passengers on deck as if it were New Year's Eve. This is what I would call a full-blown Hollywood movie-like *Bon voyage!* celebration.

It struck me as curious, as the only thing I observed all day was the arriving passengers disembarking then all the same types returning back to reboard with only their strap bags of shopping treasures. I saw no one approaching the ship looking to load travel luggage on board as if to join the cruise here in Honolulu, yours truly excepted (absent the luggage). So, who was this big *Bon Voyage!* extravaganza meant for? Moi?

Without any other way to reconcile it, I finally accepted it was for me and only me, as in my mind, I was living within a full-on Hollywood movie script anyway. Remember, it was "Y not" that got me here. All questioning aside, it was an unforgettable, adrenaline-filled moment in my life and all my friends in attendance were dancing for joy, as the music played was seemingly for our misfits group right out of Bette Davis's "Pocketful of Miracles" (1961) movie ending.

At 12:05 a.m., the ship started to slowly pull away from the dock to leave the terminal complex and make its way out to the open sea. I lingered on the deck, the smell of the open ocean enveloping me as a strong breeze blew into my face. The ship rocked ever so slightly in the waves and the stars above me shone like diamonds. *World, here I come. Absolutely nothing can get in my way now!*

Well, on that point, I was almost right.

# CHAPTER XIV

# Meeting God on a Ship

*"Only those who risk going too far can
possibly find out how far they can go."*

—*T.S. Eliot*

THE **SS CANBERRA** truly was a city on water. Launched
from a shipyard in 1961 from Belfast, Ireland, she was built
for P&O Cruise Lines to hold more than 2,000 passengers and nearly 900 crew members. The round-the-world
ship's ultimate destination was the same as its initial place
of departure: Southampton, England. As for her looks, to
me, she was as pretty as Lady Godiva naked on horseback;
and as I heard one English bloke say as we were pulling
away, she's a sleek white behemoth that can slice through
the open seas at top speeds of up to fifty miles per hour.

In 1982, the Canberra was requisitioned to transport
British soldiers to the Falklands War. Despite her size,
Argentine pilots never targeted her when she was anchored
off the South American coast, aiming their fire instead at
military destroyers and frigates. It's thought that the Argen-

tines mistook her for a hospital ship. After the war, she was celebrated as a natural treasure and ticket sales for passage on-board her boomed, but only for a short time, and her age and high costs finally put her out of commission in 1997.

Canberra's curse was that she was born in the waning glory days of the cruise industry, just as cheap plane travel was onsetting and thus, overtaking ship travel as the prime way to get out and see the world. She was the last—and the biggest and brightest—of a dying breed, clinging proudly to old Continental traditions of courtesy, stateliness, and manners. The kind of old-fashioned place where the dining room settings had more varieties of knives, forks, and spoons than I've got fingers, and where people sipped sherry in the smoking room after dinner and pretended to like it. Her customers, who mostly came from the U.K. and Australia, booked passage on her to be treated like royalty, and savor some nostalgia for the days when the sun never set on the British Empire.

Then I entered the equation—a wandering, "happy to be going along for the ride" Virginia boy who was on his way for his first time around the world, all decided on a whim and a wink, leaving behind all the grandeur that Honolulu's Chinatown had to offer. Once the lights of Oahu faded from the deck of the Canberra, a feeling of euphoria washed over me. *I did it! I'm on my way to Southampton, England, oh baby!* I felt like solid 24-carat gold. If they could mint 25 carats, I would have been a 25. Then another thought struck me: *Now what?*

I wandered the common areas of the ship for a while, marveling at what I saw—polished brass everywhere, sparkling wooden railings, and deep, rich wooden paneled walls.

I went up and down levels until I came upon a cocktail lounge where I promptly sat down and ordered myself a drink. I wondered how much it was going to cost me, as I considered the entirety of my life savings—all $15 of it—sitting in my wallet.

I sat there on my stool for quite a while, taking sips from my drink and watching the crowd slowly fill the room, even though the time was well past midnight and most of the people onboard seemed past retirement age. I struck up conversations with a few of the people around me. One gentleman told me how he had taken the Canberra's round-the-world cruise a couple of times. In the corner, a semi-talented lounge singer sat at the piano, performing easy-listening songs for the crowd. He reminds me now of Bill Murray in those old "Saturday Night Live" skits. I couldn't help but laugh when I looked in his direction.

Last call arrived around 2:00 a.m., and as good fortune would have it, one of my new friends at the bar—a physician, who was enjoying his retirement and sharing talk and drinks with me—signed for my tab. As everyone slowly filed to their cabins, I staggered out, as drunk as a lord, suddenly realizing that I needed a place to sleep.

My mind turned to that early Marx Brothers movie, "Monkey Business" in which, the four Marx Brothers were stowaways on an ocean voyage to America and get caught up with some gangsters. The whole time, they're hiding from the ship's crew and sleeping in the life rafts at night. I figured I could arrange the same type of secret living accommodations for a while.

On the Canberra, the lifeboats were hung about four feet from the railings along the promenade deck. Each was covered in thick canvas cinched tight by a rope that was pulled through a metal eye ring in the middle. Before bedding down in one, I spent about twenty minutes walking the entire perimeter of the deck, making sure no one would see me. Once I was sure the coast was clear, the time now close to 3:00 a.m., I picked out a lifeboat, climbed onto the railing in my tennis shoes, and tipped myself onto the lifeboat's canvas cover.

If I had fallen into the water, no one would have ever known about it. End of story. I'd still be on the missing list, my parents none the wiser of what happened to their long-lost son. Just as the dangers of jumping onto a boxcar at an early age didn't occur to me, neither did spilling off the railing of a cruise ship climbing onto a lifeboat at age twenty-one. Once safely in position, I reached for the rope holding the cover in place and tried to untie the knot that kept it cinched into place. I couldn't budge the damned thing, though. The cover was as tight as a drum.

I jumped back onto the deck and made my way to the next lifeboat. Same problem. I back jumped onto the deck again and this time, twisted in the air and lost my balance. *Thunk!* I landed flat on my back, and man, did I hurt! I must have been crumpled on the deck for a good five minutes. Afterward, as the pain subsided, I walked around the deck until I found a lifeboat with a looser-looking rope. I jumped on top and—using all my strength—began to massage it, encourage it, threaten it, cuss at it, and eventually, loosen it until I could create a slight opening between the cover and the life raft. But the gap wasn't big enough for me to climb through, so I moved on.

Eventually, I struck upon a lifeboat with a visibly loose enough rope for me to make a sizable opening in the cover. I was physically and mentally exhausted by this point, but I summoned my last bit of strength to raise the canvas enough to fit a person. I leaned over the gap to try to climb through it and was hit with the foulest air you could ever imagine. It completely assaulted me. It smelled like dead bird carcasses, rancid water, mildew, and sewage, fermented into one foul package. I never even saw inside the lifeboat because the smell knocked me back awkwardly onto the deck of the ship. This didn't feel like Hollywood, and it sure wasn't funny like the Marx brothers.

Beaten up, bruised, and defeated, I finally decided the lifeboats weren't going to work. Yet I needed to sleep and establish some kind of a refuge. I walked through a set of doors leading to the ship's interior and consulted a map. It told me that the lowest decks, below the promenade deck in the economy classes, all had publicly accessible bathrooms located in the hallways outside the staterooms.

With no other reasonable options, I took the elevator to the lowest deck, *G* deck, of the ship and walked the length of it. The place was as quiet as a casket. The connecting hallways were lined with maybe one hundred or so public bathrooms. They consisted of a sink, toilet, and shower. At the foot of each shower was a mini bathtub— not suitable for anyone taller than three feet to lie in.

Funny thing about the *G* deck: the state rooms were along each side of the ship; none were interior, and the hallways of all the open-use bathrooms were perpendicular thereto. Now, if you've ever been on any kind of boat or ship, doors are not left free to swing. The import of that statement is that there were approximately one hundred doors hinged with a brass hook to stay open. I couldn't just randomly choose one of these "bathtub hideaways" to sleep in without ultimately being found by the shriek of someone not understanding why I'm snoring in a three-foot tub with my clothes on. No matter how tired I was, I recognized I had only one choiceless option. I had to un-brass-hook one hundred doors before I could rest. Then it became a matter of a one-in-a-hundred chance that an awakened passenger, needing to use the loo, would pick my door.

The time was 4:30 a.m. by that point. My back hurt, my arms hurt, and hell, even my eyelashes hurt. I proceeded to try to fall asleep in one of the tubs of the bathrooms in the center of the third hallway. Cramming my legs against one of the shower walls, I climbed into the tub and closed my eyes, and for the next three hours, slept like the dead.

I'm not sure what woke me exactly, but I was jolted out of sleep. I opened my eyes, and climbed out of the tub, my whole body aching from the contortions of fitting into the footbath tub space. My watch informed me that the time was 7:30 a.m. *Well shit, the sun must be up. Time to investigate!* I could've used a few more hours of sleep, but the risk of someone walking in on me was too great. I stretched like a creaky eighty-year-old man, opened the door, and slipped into the hallway. I heard no human sounds—because people on a cruise have no good reason to get out of bed that early. Most of them were probably still drunk and wouldn't even reach the hangover stage for another few hours.

With nowhere else to go, I rode the elevator back to the promenade deck and settled onto a super comfortable leather couch in the library. For quite a while, I gazed out the picture window onto the blue, white tipped foam as we cut through the magnificently brilliant Pacific ocean—the romantic seas captured in Cary Grant movies, and Rodgers and Hammerstein musicals. Watching such a beautiful, peaceful scene while sitting on such a comfortable couch would make any reasonable person sleepy. Well, I'm nothing if not a reasonable person, so I dozed.

Waking me from my reverie was a friendly man in his early forties. He wore white shoes, white shorts, and a white shirt—with black-and-gold boards adorning his shoulders. The name tag on his chest said, "Nigel" or "Alistair" or "Laurence" or something equally English sounding. He kind of looked like a very distinguished ice cream man.

Nigel/Alistair/Laurence said, "Good morning, sir! How are you today?"

"I'm doing jolly well! Thank you for asking!" I replied, quickly sitting upright with the copy of *War and Peace* resting on my lap.

"It's a beautiful day, isn't it?" he asked.

"Jolly right! This is one of my favorite places to enjoy the morning! Just sitting here and watching the sea."

"I love this spot, too," he said, then settled onto the couch next to me. We shared a wonderful conversation for the next half-hour or so. We joked around, and I listened to some of his life stories. I felt like a kid again, hitchhiking home and witnessing the testimonials of some interesting driver who had just picked me up. It was a wonderfully comfortable occasion.

Finally, he came around to asking about me. "How long have you been on board?"

"Oh, I got on in Honolulu," I said, keeping no pretenses.

"And where are you going?"

"All the way to Southampton, England!" I replied.

"Oh, good show!" he said, checking his watch, and then standing up to leave. "I've got to be somewhere promptly at 8:00. We should have a drink later."

"By all means, we should!" I replied.

"Very good. What's your stateroom? I'll gather you up."

By this time, Nigel/Alistair/Laurence seemed like a friend, so I decided to confide in him. "Well, funny thing about that. I don't have a room."

Telling the truth wasn't hard. I knew that if I was going to actually make it around the world on the ship, I would need to come clean and find legitimate work on board at some point, anyway. There was no reason to waste time or play games before getting started. Upon hearing my confession, my new friend thought I was kidding.

"Americans!" he exclaimed. "Truly, what's your room number?"

"I'm telling you, I don't have a room."

His toothy smile vanished, as fast as if someone had flipped the *off* switch on his face. "Are you saying you're a . . . a . . . a . . . " He paused for a moment and said the word softly but clearly: "Stowaway?"

"Yeah. I'd say that's pretty close to it. But look here. I can wash dishes. I can shine shoes. I can scrape barnacles off the hull. You tell me what you need. I'm an accountant by trade, so if you need any help in the financial office, I can do that too. I'm sort of here to work my way around the world."

I didn't understand how gravely he took the situation. I thought of our conversation as a sort of job interview. He didn't. "Sir! No. You must follow me,"

he said.

"Sounds good," I said, thinking everything could easily be straightened out over a pleasant conversation with someone in charge. "I'm fine with that. Where are we going?"

"We're going to the ship's officer. I've got to turn you in!"

The ship's officer. Perfect. I didn't know what a ship's officer was, but it sounded like the person who held the position would be important enough to get me squared away with a room and a job. A shower sounded nice, too. And a bite to eat. And maybe a good nap. To me, this was yet another moment of opportunity that had landed on my feet.

Of course, my new friend wasn't seeing things that way. He was walking briskly, his posture a bit more upright and official-looking than it had been when we first met. I practically had to break into a jog to keep up with him. We walked up a series of steps—he didn't take the guest elevator, which struck me as odd—and down several long corridors until we reached the ship's bridge, at the very top.

He then opened the door and told me, "You stand here."

I did as I was instructed and stood as still as a tombstone. The bridge area looked just like you'd picture one on TV: a giant steering wheel in the center, in front of massive windows offering views of the decks below and the sea around us. On a clear day, it was said that you could see seventeen miles into the horizon while standing on the bridge, which stood more than one hundred feet above the water line. It was just spectacular. Around me, a crew, all in clean, perfectly pressed uniforms scurried about, focusing their attention on all sorts of knobs and buttons and navigational devices and . . . me.

A few minutes later, my escort returned with a man who looked slightly older than the rest of the men on the bridge, but not quite middle-aged, and his uniform had a few more gold bars on the shoulders. He was the officer in charge on the bridge—and as the ship's first mate, meaning he was second in command to the captain. At that time, moment, and place as he stood in front of me, he was God on the SS Canberra.

He spoke to me in a nobleman's British accent. "My ensign here tells me you've stowed away on the ship." I couldn't quite read the expression on his face, but he didn't seem angry or alarmed. Maybe more like a little intrigued, or even slightly amused. He seemed like a man of reason. "Yes. I got on in Honolulu." I then explained my dream to travel around the world, and how excited I was to have the opportunity to be on the ship. I repeated that I would be happy to work in any capacity to earn my keep. I kept a smile on my face as I explained everything, and for a second he smiled back, before quickly snapping back into his God of the Ship pose. I could still see a sense of humor twinkling in his eyes, though.

"Well sir," he told me, politely as can be, as if we were sitting over a pot of tea, "that's not exactly how it's done. I'm going to have to sort this out. May I see your passport?"

"Funny thing about that . . . passport. I don't have one," I said.

"Well, do you have any form of identification?"

"Of course!" I said. "I've got a driver's license." I gladly handed it over to him, and he examined it closely.

"Well . . . Mr. Van Cleve, if you would be so kind as to stand here with my ensign, I'll be back shortly."

"Terrific," I said.

The man disappeared around a corner, leaving me with another ensign—who was a kid maybe in his early twenties in a ship's uniform—but for only about two minutes. I enjoyed the bridge view while I waited. It really was spectacular. The sun was rising over the ocean, and I felt like it was the dawn of a new, wonderful experience. I wonder if my state room will have a window. Will they give me a roommate?

He returned with two men by his side. "Would you escort this man down?" he said.

The two men nodded and snapped into position. One stood in front of me, and the other took position in back. "Good day to you, Mr. Van Cleve," the officer said.

"Good day to you, too," I replied cheerily, and walked off the bridge with my two escorts.

I should have known something was amiss by this point, but I didn't. It's not that I was being foolish about my situation. Instead, I was just overly optimistic. I still adamantly choose to look on the positive side of things, no matter what events might befall me. My philosophy is that we're on this planet for too short a time to do otherwise.

My two escorts led me down and across a new series of stairwells and hallways, until we reached the ship's infirmary. *This is strange*, I thought. I had expected to be led to the crew's quarters to learn about my new job. Instead, I was marched past a pretty nurse who gave me a friendly, but confused look, through the patient treatment area, and into a small room with a bed and two portholes.

*This must be the only room they've got open*, I realized. They closed the door behind me, but I didn't pay much attention. I was too busy assessing my new quarters. I sauntered to the portholes and pressed my nose against one to admire the magnificent blue Pacific Ocean splashing against the hull. Two whole portholes! Then I looked at the inviting single bed. I hopped on it, crossing my feet, and propping my head on the pillow. The mattress felt as comfortable as a cloud. *And no roommates! Holy shit! I can't believe I've made it! I'm on the road, baby! I'm going around the world!*

If I had looked carefully, I would have noticed that the door had no doorknob on the inside. I was imprisoned. This room was the ship's mental health ward, and for me, it doubled as the brig. Even though the Canberra was the world's largest luxury liner, it had no steel barred brig. Apparently, the owners didn't expect any white-haired British pensioners taking round-the-world cruises to get unruly enough to need one. Me: alone, sleep-deprived, locked up, passport-less, almost penniless, knowing no one and completely unaware of my surroundings, and on the high seas . . . I couldn't have been happier. I closed my eyes with a smile on my face and snoozed, blissfully unaware of the hornet's nest I had just kicked.

# CHAPTER XV

# Royalty is for Country Boys, Too

*"If you don't get out of the box you've been raised in, you won't understand how much bigger the world is."*

*—Angelina Jolie*

**I'M NOT SURE** how long I had been sleeping before the door to my stateroom—or the mental health ward, whatever you'd prefer to call it—slammed open, and two gentlemen were suddenly inside it. They were wearing the same Popeye suits as much of the rest of the crew, but after opening my bleary eyes, I noticed something different: they had holsters on their belts, each carrying a revolver.

"Sir, your presence is requested with the captain," one of the two men said, as politely as if he was a waiter serving me a Mai Thai with an umbrella in it beside the pool.

I accepted the kind invitation and was once again marched through the ship's maze of hallways and stairways. Eventually, I was led through a doorway that opened into a spacious reception area, which I realized must lead to the captain's office. The setup was as fancy as a peacock feather—all gold trim, with thick carpeting and stately mahogany furniture. About what you would expect the waiting room of a man of high position to be like. I looked out the porthole and could see that the sun was casting soft, late-afternoon shadows.

There were three chairs beside the receptionist's desk, and the guards placed me in the middle one. They sat, too, on either side of me. I tried to strike up a conversation with them, but they stayed stone-faced and didn't pay any attention, like they were auditioning to be one of those guards at Buckingham Palace. Not that I minded. I figured that in a very few minutes, I was going to be sharing a few good laughs with the captain, and everything would be alright.

The silence was broken by the phone ringing on the receptionist's desk. She answered, and after a couple of short words, motioned for me to enter the captain's office— so I did, with one armed Buckingham wannabe standing in front of me, and the other behind. What happened next was so Hollywood I couldn't believe my eyes—like straight out of a James Bond movie. Oh, I stand corrected. The James Bond film, "Diamonds Are Forever," starring Sean Connery, which was in fact, partially filmed on board the Canberra in 1971.

I walked into the room to face an oversized desk. Positioned behind it was a giant leather chair, with the back facing me. I settled into one of two wooden chairs in front of the desk, and one of the guards dropped in the other. After a few dramatically quiet moments, the chair swiveled around, and sitting in it was the captain. He was a portly man in his late fifties, with graying, receding hair who—I kid you not—was wearing an eyepatch. The guy looked downright diabolical. I was half-expecting a white cat to be resting in his lap, and for him to tell me about his evil plan to take over the world. I'd prefer not to use his real name, so I'll just call him Captain Blight.

"Sir," he said, glaring at me out of his good eye and making a face like he had just eaten something rotten, "I understand that you're a . . . " He paused for added effect, " . . . stowaway."

"Well, yes, sir. I guess that's the best description so far. But I'm here to work myself around the world," I said, and then listed, for the third time, the many jobs I'd be willing to do on the ship, including barnacle scraping. "I'm really anxious to see what you have available." Blight shook his head. "Well, sir, do you realize that when you're on this ship, you're on British soil? And since you've entered the soil of a sovereign country, you will need to show me your passport."

"Funny thing about that . . . passport," I said, yet again explaining that I didn't possess one.

"I'll ask you again," the captain said. "Where is your passport?"

"Well, there wasn't time. I never considered it. I've never gotten a passport. I've never left America before."

This was a true "Cool Hand Luke" moment. If you've ever seen the movie, you know what I mean. Paul Newman's character in it is a well-meaning, good-natured guy, convicted of a minor, victimless crime. He's sentenced to two years in prison and is forced to work on a Florida chain gang, under an evil warden who's a stickler for rules. Luke, who has an independent streak, is constantly being punished. In one of the most famous Hollywood scenes ever, the warden says to him, "What we have here is failure to communicate."

Blight and I clearly had failure to communicate. He thought I was lying about my passport, but I wasn't. "Well then . . . sir." He paused between words, as if maybe Van Cleve wasn't truly even my last name. "Where's your luggage?"

I was starting to get the sense that maybe things were going differently than I had expected. "Well, funny thing about that. This was such an unplanned trip, like I said, and it came about so fast, there really was no time to pack."

"Sir!" he sputtered. "You expect me to believe that you're about to go on a 20,000-mile journey and you have packed no luggage?"

I replied, respectfully, "Yup, no luggage." His mouth tightened and his bushy eyebrows dropped. He wasn't buying it—even though it was true. Blight, in his very dignified British way, then told me in no uncertain terms to stop this nonsense and tell him the truth, now (fist pounding on desk).

"Tell me now, sir. Where is your luggage? Because one way or another, I will find it." Being the logical man that he was, he figured that I absolutely had to have brought luggage with me, like any other sane human being would—even a stowaway. And inside that suitcase would be my passport. Because who tries to travel the world without a passport? The answer, of course, was me, but he refused to believe it.

"Honestly, I walked on board with only the clothes on my back," I told him, earnestly trying to ease the tension, but with no success. Instead, he just got madder and madder, and his face grew red as a pickled beet. So much steam came out of his ears, you could've thought he was a tea kettle. I wasn't trying to get on his bad side, though. Truly.

"We're going to take you back, now," he said to me, then turned his icy one-eyed gaze to the security officer sitting next to me. "Take this young man back." Apparently the only opening he had on the ship for me was the brig!

The two officers did just that, and led me back through the infirmary, past the friendly nurse, and into the mental health ward—otherwise known as my temporary stateroom, or more accurately, my cell. I was beginning to feel more like Cool Hand Luke with every second.

From what I was told later, the captain's search for my phantom luggage—and the phantom passport within it—began immediately after I was taken back to my quarters. He set teams of crew members to search every corner of every public space on the ship, from bow to stern, top to bottom. Considering the Canberra was the size of a small city neighborhood, the search was bound to take several days and require multiple shifts of multiple searchers, but Blight didn't care. Meanwhile, I sat in my room for the rest of that afternoon and into the evening, looking out the two portholes until darkness fell. My stomach rumbled constantly because they didn't feed me at all that entire first day, and my only company was the copy of *War and Peace*, still by my side. Finally, sometime later, I fluffed up my two wonderful pillows, rolled over and went into the most peaceful of deep sleep. Despite my circumstances and imprisonment, my sunny optimism never dimmed. I was convinced that everything would turn out well. And even if it didn't, the ship was moving, and we were on the open seas. I was headed West. Always West; now West by Southwest.

Around seven o'clock the next morning, my side-armed

friends opened the door and greeted me with a, "Please follow us, sir."

As if I had a choice, I agreed. Once again, they took me through the maze, following a different course, which ended with a set of steep stairs that led us down to the crew's mess— which is the eating area and general gathering spot for the crew between shifts. At that moment, there were maybe sixty crew members milling about, eating breakfast or lingering on the benches of the long picnic tables that filled the room. The guards introduced me to Seamus, a man in his late thirties dressed in stained white pants and a white shirt. He was the chief of the crew's mess.

"We're delivering Mr. Van Cleve to you, Seamus," one of the guards said.

"Please see that he is fed properly and let us know when we should come back and collect him."

Food! Now we're getting somewhere. I hadn't eaten in roughly 36 hours, and the smells of the food being served, were almost overwhelming. I was practically ready to grab bacon and eggs off a serving tray and eat them with my bare hands.

I peered toward Seamus, and he stood stone-faced until the guards climbed back up the stairs. Then he turned to me, "Oh my God! You're the stowaway!" he exclaimed, slapping me on the back like a long-lost friend.

"Yeah. Why?" I said.

"You're the greatest person I've ever met in my life! Tell me what you're doing here!"

I explained for the fourth time how I got on board and explained again about how I was willing to perform any work at all, all the way down to barnacle scraping. He asked when the last time was that I ate, and I told him.

"You must be ravished!" he exclaimed.

"I am."

"What would you like?" Seamus asked.

"Well, you got any bacon?"

"Bacon?" he said. "We've got better than that. We have access to everything the guests are served in the dining room upstairs. Whatever they're eating, we're eating. Do you like lobster?"

"I love lobster!"

He yelled to someone in the kitchen staff nearby, "Lobster and eggs for . . ." He turned to me. "What's your first name?" I told him. "Lobster and eggs for Guy, then!" he said. A couple of men suddenly jumped into action to make Seamus's orders happen.

"Well, can I have a couple of pieces of bacon, too?"

"Of course. And sausage. Would you like some sausage?"

"Sounds great!" I said like a morbidly obese king with a table full of delights before him. By this time, a small crowd began to gather around us. I sat at an empty picnic table as a feast was placed in front of me. As I ate, some of the crew members joined me at the table and told me they had been looking forward to meeting me—like I was a movie star in their midst, or something. They were as giddy as stadium audiences when the Beatles broke into the first song of their set.

Within the first couple of minutes of our interactions, I learned two vital pieces of information: 1) Almost everyone thought Captain Blight was a complete bastard, and 2) Blight was already going absolutely bonkers over the search for my luggage and passport. Every time a search crew would report back to him empty handed, he would berate them incessantly.

Within the first ten minutes of our interactions, I had already made a dozen new friends. Within thirty minutes, my stomach was full to the point of almost bursting my belt buckle. The crew was determined to make up for Blight's mistreatment of me by stuffing me like a Christmas turkey. Someone even presented me with a set of Heinz A-1 and ketchup bottles, but instead of being filled with steak sauce or ketchup, they had good old-fashioned hooch in them. Some contained rum, others gin, others vodka, and so on. The crew kept them in the bottles as contraband. Seamus asked me what mixers I liked with my drinks, and I replied "ginger ale, tonic and Coca-Cola," so he placed a couple of cans of each in front of me.

"We're changing shifts here in a moment, and I'm going to have to move on to other duties. I'll call the guards and get them back here for you, but take these drinks with you, so you can enjoy them."

"Yes, sir!" I replied.

He vanished and within a few minutes, I was marching back to the mental health ward with my two armed escorts. They didn't seem to care that I was cradling enough alcohol, stowed together in an oversized napkin, to put 10 sailors three sheets to the wind. Seamus must have had a conversation with them about it, and on the ship, he was their superior, rank-wise. Their lone duty as guards was simply to make sure I didn't escape somehow, and they performed it admirably.

Once again, I was walked through the infirmary, past the nurse, who was more curious than ever as she saw me walk by. With my arms full, I sweetly nodded to her because, by this point, we were developing a silent, pleasant connection, and I was once again, locked in my room.

Inside, I took a nip, two or five, from my alcohol party stash and fell pleasantly asleep.

The next thing I knew, the door was opening again, and I was being escorted to the crew's mess for a late lunch. For the second time that day, I received the celebrity treatment from the people in the room, and I started getting to know some more of them. Seamus had created a sort of assigned seating arrangement, filling my picnic table with his closest friends. The conversation was rowdy and pleasant. And filled with food. Man, I ate like royalty.

For the next couple of days, these round-trip eating adventures to the crew's mess became my routine. I'd chow and drink with them, then get sent back to my room where I would drink and sleep, and then return to eat and drink some more. On the third day, the crew gave me a small gift: a cassette player and some "Best of Rock n' Roll" tapes in a shoebox so I could listen to music between sleeping and drinking in my private room/cell. All the while, Captain Blight maintained his round-the-clock searches, with off-duty personnel, for my nonexistent luggage. The crew told me that with every hour and day that passed, he became more and more agitated. I was a problem he didn't know how to solve, and he was a man who knew how to solve every problem that arose on his ship. He did not like being powerless. Discovering my passport became his great white whale, and he was Ahab.

At first, I didn't understand his obsession with it. After all, if I had known that having a passport was such a big deal, I would have gotten mine a long time earlier. But someone from the crew informed me that if I didn't possess a passport, he couldn't just dump me off at any of the ship's ports because no country would take responsibility for me. He would possibly be stuck with me on the ship for the rest of the cruise—which was a completely unacceptable arrangement to him!

However, to me, it sounded like a completely acceptable arrangement. The one major drawback to my comfortable cell was that it did not possess a bathroom. Since I was eating and drinking so liberally, this became a small problem. To my relief, so to speak, I discovered that if I knocked on my door, the nurse would eagerly open it and allow me to use the facilities in the infirmary. The guards never stood outside the room when I occupied it because they knew I wasn't going to escape. During the course of these bathroom breaks, the nurse and I became increasing friendly as I was breaking her boredom. Then finally came the day I came out to use the loo where she became quite amorous. Due to my recent brothel graduate school training in the unbounded exchange of boy/girl reciprocal pleasures, together with being a super healthy 21-year-old male, I was able to give my new nurse friend a *once, twice, three times around the world* experience without ever leaving her infirmary. Once we called it quits, she struggled to make her way over to the infirmary's four-foot-tall green oxygen tank for both of us to share a couple of full measures of pure oxygen, as there was little left in the room.

Well-to-do elderly British cruise passengers are a surprisingly healthy lot, I discovered, and the ship's nurse could get mind numbingly bored at times. I made for an enjoyable roommate as such and was always willing to please her in any way possible. She was in her early thirties, brunette, and wore a tightly fitting nurse's white outfit. Underneath, she was fit like a showgirl wearing stringy, strappy bikini-style panties and dressed up sometimes in nurse heels to kill. The two of us had lots of time to engage in uninterrupted fun.

By the end of the week, I was frequently being joined in my quarters by many of my friends in the crew's mess. They realized that although I wasn't allowed outside of the room without an escort, they could freely enter it. The place became party central. I had music, friends, booze, and a sexy, eager companion. The party was at the Mental Health Ward and life was perfect! Even under the nose of Blight. No one bothered to tell the captain anything about my comfortable living. He thought I was suffering in solitary confinement. All the while, he kept increasing the number of crew members searching the ship for my passport and suitcase, which he just *knew* would eventually be found. The two groups of roving searchers were increased to three, and then it got to the point that every off-shift crew member had to spend some time each day searching the ship, stem-to-stern.

He became so incensed at the failure to turn up a single clue as to my luggage and passports' whereabouts that by the fifth day of my voyage, he ordered the search of all passenger staterooms as well. Crew members were opening people's drawers and closets, searching under their beds, leaving no stone unturned, much to the annoyance and confusion of the paying passengers. Blight was damned if he wasn't going to find some way to get rid of me.

During my meal trips to the crew's mess, I became friends with a radio operator named Peter. He told me that the captain had ordered him to contact every port between our current location and Southampton, to request permission to dump me off. Each call proved unsuccessful, and he hadn't yet found a country willing to take responsibility for me because I didn't have a passport. Peter was thoroughly amused by how each failed attempt riled the captain. Blight was getting madder than a bobcat freshly caught in a cage.

Meanwhile, I was living the life! After maybe a week passed—it's hard to tell because the days and nights blended so beautifully—I was holding court at my usual crew's mess picnic table seat, readying for another kingly meal when Peter stood up to address the crowd.

"Hey mates, guess what? Guy's with us all the way to Southampton!" he declared. "I just finished calling each and every port, and not one of them will accept responsibility. He's with us till the end!"

A rousing cheer went up from the crowd. It was unbelievable, they were acting like they had just won the lottery. I was touched by the emotion and incredibly excited. It seemed only logical now that Blight would put me to work, instead of punishing me. I couldn't wait to find out what I'd be doing to earn my keep. During the rowdy celebration of my new status, Seamus pulled me into a corner and draped his arm around my shoulder.

"We're friends," he said, "and I'm taking care of you, aren't I?" I nodded enthusiastically. "Then tell me. Where's your luggage? I won't tell the captain."

"Seamus, I swear, buddy, I didn't come on with any luggage. There was no time. I saw the chance to jump on the ship, so I jumped on the ship. I've got no passport. I've never needed one. I've never left the country!"

Seamus believed me and quickly spread the word among the crew. They didn't mind the extra work during the fruitless searches because Blight was required to pay them for it. His desperate mission was fattening their paychecks and costing him real overtime money. At the same time, the legend of me was catching like wildfire among the passengers, who were becoming increasingly curious about the mysterious stowaway who was causing the captain so much heartburn, and the reason for their cabins being searched.

The Brits love gossip as much as anyone. I was turning into a cult hero.

They were imagining all sorts of exotic explanations of who I was and how I got there. Soon enough, they would meet me in the flesh—but not exactly in the way I, or they, or Blight, expected.

Being in a cell for a majority of the day, I didn't have much of a clue on the happenings aboard the rest of the ship. I obtained tidbits of information here and there during my stints in the crew's mess or the parties in my room, but I knew very little about the happenings among my new friends who worked aboard the SS Canberra, or the thousands of passengers they served. For instance, I had no idea that Seamus shared a bottle of scotch with the commodore of the P&O Cruise Line fleet every night after his shift. This turned out to be a very important piece of information.

Though Captain Blight was the king, emperor, and chief dictator on all matters aboard the Canberra, he did have a boss: the commodore. Generally, the person who held this lofty position worked out of one of the company's headquarters in Australia. But occasionally, he traveled aboard a P&O ship, for the purpose of observing the quality of the cruise experience, and to rate the captain on his job performance. In this particular year, the commodore was traveling around the world on the Canberra, watching over the shoulder of Blight, and holding the captain's 'corporate ladder' future with the P&O Cruise Line within his oversight.

Every evening, after the ship's activities settled down, and the crew's day shift came to an end and sun extinguished into the warm Pacific, the commodore would meet Seamus at a quiet spot at the base of the smokestacks on the top deck. They would take swigs from a large bottle of finely aged scotch and share sea stories. They never missed an end of day tribute to the spirits of the sea—no matter the day or the weather. The two were best friends.

Unbeknownst to me, Seamus was giving the commodore daily updates on me, the stowaway who had snuck aboard in Hawaii and was being held in "solitary confinement," while Blight maniacally searched for my non-existent passport. The reports were like a soap opera, with a new twist added each day. The commodore loved it. Seamus believed me when I told him—truthfully—that I hadn't brought any luggage aboard and had never owned a passport, and he grew angrier and angrier with each passing day as the captain forced the crew on another frantic goose chase. He described me to the commodore, who generally stayed out of the captain's business in running the ship, because he was one of the nicest guys in the world.

"Guy doesn't mean any harm," Seamus told his friend one evening, early in the second week of my captivity. "He just innocently wanted to work his way around the world for the romance of it all."

Seamus described my living conditions harshly, as if I were being treated like an 18th century prisoner held in the dank, rat-infested, bilgewater bottom of the ship. I, on the other hand, felt like I was traveling in first class. I had a comfortable bed, a quiet room, two portholes to look out, and I was partying all the time. After our initial world-class trip around the world encounter, the nurse always left my door unlocked so I could have free access to her and the loo when needed, and I was being fed world-class meals in the crew's mess every morning, afternoon, and evening.

Passage to Southampton, England in the mental health ward had come to sound just fine to me.

Still, Seamus didn't think it was fair that I wasn't allowed to leave my room, so he used some creative license to get his point across. Beyond my living conditions, he didn't need to exaggerate about the one-eyed captain's crazy obsession with me, and the incredible expense and effort Blight was putting into the passport search so he could kick me off the ship. He described that situation in full detail to the commodore, as well.

"Guy doesn't deserve the treatment he's getting," Seamus said. The commodore nodded in agreement and said he would speak to Blight. And he did, apparently the next day.

The next morning, as I made my usual escorted walk through the ship's maze of hallways and stairwells to the crew's mess for breakfast, Seamus greeted me with a curious ear-to-ear grin.

"What's going on?" I asked cautiously.

"The commodore has arranged some new living quarters for you."

"Is that so?"

"Yes, you're being put in a suite."

"You're kidding!" I said.

"I've been talking with him about it. There's only one unoccupied room on the ship. B203. It's now yours."

"B203! Terrific!" I said. I had no idea of what the significance of B203 meant, of course. But a suite sure sounded nice.

Seamus told me that after breakfast, I would be taken back to the mental health ward to collect my belongings, then I would be shown to my new quarters. Afterward, I would be released from captivity, and given free reign of the entire ship, able to enjoy all of its luxuries and trappings, from bow to stern.

"Oh my god, that's just fabulous!" I screeched to Seamus, thanking him profusely—though I have to say that I suddenly came to realize that I wouldn't be eating meals with my friends in the crew's mess anymore, which sent a pang of regret through me.

Seamus insisted on one big condition to the new arrangement: under no circumstance was I allowed to leave the ship at any port stop before it reached

Southampton, England because I didn't have a passport.

"Sure! Absolutely fine. I understand," I said. At that time, I still didn't quite know what having a passport meant. I do now.

After breakfast, I noticed that my two armed guards had lost their arms, as they took me—without guns or holsters— back to my cell and then to B203, the happiest combination of letters and numbers I had ever heard in my life. At the door of my new suite, they told me goodbye and their entire demeanor changed. "So long," I replied, waving goodbye.

I opened the door to my suite and was blown away by the sight before me. It turns out that the letter "B" for B203 was a very important detail. All the living quarters on the ship were coded by letter. Ones that started with "A" were the most expensive and lavish—built for dukes and earls, or people who had as much money as dukes and earls. Those were all on the highest deck. Ones that started with "B" were only a small step down, intended for the comfortably wealthy, instead of the insanely rich. To me, "B" stood for "big." My stateroom had a big bathtub, a big shower, a big bed, a big sitting area, a big everything. Best of all, the room came with servants! There were three people who were assigned to B203: throughout the day and night. If I wanted a ham sandwich at any time, I could request one on a little card, and it would be brought to me, licketty split, even at 3:00 a.m.

Every time I left the room, the bed was made, the floor was vacuumed, the lamps were dusted, and the towels were changed around the sink. Each of the servants was from India, and though they didn't speak a lick of English, they did know the concept of British hospitality, and performed their mission impeccably. I didn't have a dime to my name, yet suddenly, I felt richer than a pharaoh.

As soon as I had taken full inventory of the room, I decided to explore the world's largest cruise ship for the first time since the night of my arrival on board. I closed the door behind me, placed the key in my pocket, and took advantage of my newly created freedom. I started by taking the elevator to the promenade deck and strolling among the passengers. A few of the crew spotted me and said, "Oh, you're out! How did you arrange that?"

"Seamus fixed it with the commodore so I wouldn't have to stay in the mental health ward anymore," I replied.

"Oh, that's fabulous!" they said, and began patting me on the back and shaking my hand. The scene started to attract the attention of my now fellow passengers, who suddenly realized that I was the stowaway—and the reason their cabins were repeatedly searched by Captain Blight during the past week. It was like a lightbulb went off over their heads.

One welcoming elderly couple marched straight up to me and wanted to know all the details. "Tell us, why did you do it?" they asked. As I was describing the story, they waved some of their friends over to hear and meet the "stowaway," and before I knew it, a crowd formed. Everybody wanted to know who I was, and how I got there, and so without a second of contemplation, I started shooting from the hip.

"Well, I'm traveling around the world, and writing a book about all of the places I go and the people I meet," I said. I'm not sure how I came up with that explanation, but I said it with such complete conviction my fellow passengers seemed more than agreeable to it. Eager to hear of my adventures, and to tell me of their own, a bunch of them invited me to join them at the bar. I did, and after taking a sip of my morning bloody mary cocktail, explained to them how I got on the ship.

When I was finished, they asked about my luggage and where it was hidden. I told them I had none and explained how there wasn't enough time for me to pack my belongings when the chance to walk onto the Canberra arose.

"I saw an opportunity and I took it. *Boom.* Now I'm here and going to Southampton, England, and traveling around the world." They all got a good belly laugh out of my explanation. Everyone seemed delighted at the chance to see, meet, and hear the legendary stowaway. In short order, I was like George Clooney at a sorority party—and everyone wanted a piece of my time. The more the liquor flowed, the friendlier the Brits became. I must have been introduced to a couple hundred people that day, as I retold my story during lunch, throughout the afternoon and all the way till and through dinner. Everywhere I moved on the ship, people approached me to shake my hand and exchange a few good-natured words, like, "At least our cabins don't need to be searched anymore!" Or, "Oh my goodness, you really snookered the captain, didn't you?"

I didn't really snooker the captain. I was simply my earnest, friendly self, and had suddenly found myself in a pretty magnificent suite and living quite large. Many of my fellow passengers asked how I planned to support myself on the ship—even just to pay my bar tab. I told them that I didn't know. Some then started slipping me cash and saying things like, "Well here's 5 quid for your troubles." Or 10 quid. Or even 20 quid. I couldn't believe their generosity. By the time my cruise ended, I had more than £1,500 in my pocket, all in cash handed me by my fellow passengers, unsolicited.

Every day, I learned, and was surprised to learn, the bounties of my voyage. I give you the equator. For all sailors (even accidental sailors), the first time one crosses the equator is a matter of great celebration. Of course, this fact was brought to my attention by the loving crew, and it was yet one more occasion to show me a grand time. I was invited to the Pigsty. The Pigsty was the crew's nightclub lounge, completely off-limits to passengers, hidden below deck near the ship's bow. It looked like an old-fashioned British pub meets "Saturday Night Fever." The scene there was perfect for all and any occasions, and it was perfect for the crew this night to hold the special sailor's ceremony for the time-honored passage of a sailor's first equator crossing.

The ceremony was comprised of a twenty-one-gun salute. However, in lieu of guns, they lined up twenty-one shots of your preferred liquor to mark the moment. My liquor of choice was Stolichnaya vodka. Music, dance, attaboys, back-slapping, and cheers made up this once-in-a-lifetime occasion. Somewhere after the eighteenth shot, *I* was shot. However, I have it on the good authority that I did, indeed, drink all twenty-one shots. Part One of their ceremony for me was then followed by a Part Two.

Part Two was where Seamus and about six of my closest crew friends, arm-in-arm, took me to the highest point of the ship for a moment of deep reflection. Our troop stumbled (with an occasional fall or two) to the summit of the highest flat point of the ship, which was alongside one of the smokestacks. We all laid on the flat of our backs, looking up at the midnight symphony of stars above us. Breathlessly, it was apparent why we were here. On a clear night, as you're passing over the equator going from North to South Pacific, you can see no dark in the sky. The stars are so abundant that they all melded together as if there was a single light shining from horizon to horizon, casting a shadow from your raised arm, like the sun itself was shining. To this day, I am still affected by that moment.

# CHAPTER XVI

# Saved by the King of Tonga

*"When a man is a traveler, the world is his home
and the sky is his roof, where he hangs his hat is
his home and all the people are his family."*

—*Drew Bundini Brown*

**OVER THE NEXT** several days, as the passengers throughout the ship got to know me, I transformed in their eyes from being the "mysterious stowaway" to being "Guy, the fellow who is writing the book about his adventures."

I loved every minute of my long encounters with fellow passengers because so many of them had lived such interesting lives. Some of their stories stick with me to this day. Others, I was too drunk to recall. Even though, at age twenty-one, I could hold my liquor pretty well, I was no match for the Brits when it came to sitting at a bar and sharing yarns over drinks.

One of the more remarkable people I met was an older gentleman who fought the Germans in North Africa in World War II. He came from a privileged family yet volunteered to serve on the front lines. He grew to love that region of the world in his time there, and after the war, he became a game warden at a massive wildlife refuge. Most of his job involved chasing off dangerous poachers to protect the animals—and in the line of duty he had been kidnapped, drugged, beaten, and shot. He showed me three different gunshot wounds on his body.

The man truly moved me. The image of his face is still so clear—the leathery, dark, sun-tanned skin, and more lines than on a topographical map across his face. He grew a prim-and-proper mustache on his upper lip and had a full head of silver hair that most men half his age would envy. I listened to him for hours one afternoon as he told stories, while I scratched occasional notes on napkins. Sadly, I lost track of what I had written, but the impression he made on me, and what he told me about his life and experiences in the African animal kingdom, are as clear four decades later as they were when I walked the decks of the SS Canberra.

Another similarly amazing person I met was a British woman who volunteered as a nurse during World War II. She was sent to France and then into Germany, near the end of hostilities, and was given the grim task of patching up badly injured and mentally decimated soldiers. After the war, she founded a hospital. She, like the game warden, tapped into my soul. If I had been locked in the mental health ward with no other human contact, given only bread and water for the rest of the cruise, I still would have considered the experience a success simply by comparison to the pain and agony suffered by those I was lucky enough to then meet. Considering the lots they had to endure throughout their lives, it was the ultimate honor to be able to converse with them about it now.

There were so many other interactions on the ship that made me laugh, cry, or something in-between. Most of my meetings were such a blur. Everyone was so generous in offering me libations, and so eager to capture my attention, that I had to find creative excuses for escaping the bar and catching a sober breath—not to mention to give my liver a break. When I got the chance, I'd walk the decks, or spend some time resting alongside one of the swimming pools.

In those brief moments by myself, I would think about just how lucky I was to be enjoying this exotic and luxurious experience. Only six months earlier, I had never in my life so much as crossed the Mississippi.

One afternoon, the ship crossed the Tropic of Cancer. The crew alerted everyone beforehand because the event is always considered a big one. At the precise time of the crossing, nearly all the passengers celebrated on the sun deck, where the chef had set up a massive lunch buffet for everyone to enjoy. I, on the other hand, dove into one of the ship's swimming pools. The pools were set up so they were filled with fresh sea water constantly pumped (and filtered) from the Pacific, so there was no need for using chemicals in them. As the announcement came over the loudspeakers, "We are now crossing the Tropic of Cancer," I dove headfirst into one of the pools and slowly swam in the ocean water from one side of the pool to the other.

In other words, at twenty-one, I got to swim across the Tropic of Cancer.

Later, on the cruise, I got to swim across the equator the same way. And then did the same thing with the International Date Line, going from a Wednesday to a Thursday at 1:00 in the afternoon. How many other twenty-one-year-olds can say they've done that?

Most of the passengers regarded me as a swashbuckling hero—and with every good hero story, there needs to be a villain. In their eyes, that role went to Captain Blight. They were angry over his needless search for my luggage and of my initial imprisonment. The crew, who were also largely on my side, stoked the fire with the passengers, and their demeanor toward him became icy.

On every cruise ship, it's considered an honor for a passenger to be invited to sit at the captain's table for dinner in the dining room. But the friction aboard the Canberra rose so high that none of the passengers wanted to accept Blight's invitation. Instead, they all wanted to sit with me, at one of the larger dining tables. The captain never acknowledged me, or even looked in my direction, as far as I could tell. From what the crew told me, though, he was hopping mad at the slight, and became more set on kicking me off the ship than ever, especially after the Tonga incident.

The Kingdom of Tonga is a chain of nearly 2,000 Polynesian islands—of which only a few dozen are inhabited—spread across a stretch of ocean about the size of Texas. It lies about two-thirds of the way between Hawaii and New Zealand and was known as the "Friendly Islands" by Westerners because of the welcoming reception received by Captain James Cook upon his arrival in the 18th century. The main island is Tongatapu – a hilly, magnificent protrusion of tropical forests rising above the sea on a fertile bed of rich volcanic ash. It's where almost three quarters of Tonga's then 20,000 citizens lived, and is home to Tonga's capital city, Nuku'alofa.

During most of the 20th century, Tonga was protected by the British while maintaining its own sovereignty but severed all dependence in 1970. Chiefs have ruled the country for the past 800 years, but in 1975, it became a constitutional monarchy, with a king as head of state and commander in chief of the military. To this day, Tonga's royal family still rules and is revered by the people.

The Canberra arrived at Tongatapu nearing my second week aboard. I watched with awe from the top decks as the ship navigated through a channel populated with tiny, gorgeous islands until we reached the port of Nuku'alofa. Once again, fate had blessed me with an amazing sight to behold, and I was tremendously grateful. One of my fellow passengers told me that Captain Blight had planned a special reception and dinner for the King of Tonga aboard the ship for that very evening.

The event was an annual tradition, held when the ship came to the country's tiny capital anchor port, and the locals considered it a huge social occasion. Because seats were limited in the special reception area, only a select list of well-connected, high-society, A-deck passengers received invitations from the captain to attend. Fortunately, I had become friends with many of them, and one informed me that he had made arrangements for me to go to the party as his guest.

"You should go! It's going to be fabulous!" he said. "It's probably the best event on this whole cruise."

"Well, what's the dress?" I asked.

"It's coat-and-tie, of course."

I reminded my friend that I didn't have a coat or tie—or a shirt, slacks, or shoes to go with them. "Not to worry," he said. "I'll treat you to some new clothes!"

My friend sent me to the clothing shop, where a man measured my arms, neck, legs, and chest, then within minutes, magically handed me a set of perfectly fitting clothes worthy of being worn in front of a king. I looked in the full-length mirror and could barely recognize myself. I had been transformed from Virginia country boy to British high society, like I was a male version of Eliza Doolittle in "My Fair Lady."

The time of the reception arrived soon afterward, and the pomp and circumstance surrounding the King of Tonga's arrival was even more impressive than I imagined it would be. He was paddled out to the ship in a Polynesian canoe and arrived wearing full traditional regalia, including a headdress, and flowing, colorful robes. The crew led the king into the ship's ballroom, where a throne was set up on a podium for him to sit while receiving the one hundred or so passengers, including myself, who were allowed to attend the event. To my surprise, Captain Blight was nowhere to be found. Word had filtered through the crew that he was still so incensed over my presence onboard, and the passengers' hostility toward him, that he had by now, mostly sequestered himself in his office and quarters and preferred not to be seen by anyone. So instead, the Commodore performed the honor of welcoming the King of Tonga aboard, on behalf of the SS Canberra and the P&O Cruise Line.

The reception truly was fit for a king. There was a band playing on the stage, an open bar, and a tremendous buffet of every kind of finger food, roasted, sautéed vegetable, soufflé, and every fruit-filled pastry and dessert imaginable. After the food and many drinks were served, a reception line was set up for each guest to meet the king as he sat on the throne. Naturally, I took my place in it, but at the end of the line. I couldn't believe I was about to shake the hand of the royal head of state of a sovereign nation.

The king was a big Polynesian man who, by the time I had reached him in line, had indulged himself with quite a bit of liquor.

"Hi, my name is Guy Van Cleve. I'm from the USA," I said. He extended his massive right hand, and it practically swallowed mine when we shook. I lingered for an extra second, the reason for my being at the end of the reception line, hoping to make a personal connection with him the way I did with every new person I met—regardless of their status or rank.

"I couldn't help noticing as we arrived here on the ship this one particular little island. It was the most beautiful island I've ever seen in my life," I said. The king smiled and nodded, appreciating the flattery.

"I'm curious," I continued. "Are you in a position that you could sell one of these islands to someone? To a private citizen like me, maybe?"

He let out a deep, friendly laugh that practically shook the ballroom chandeliers. "Oh my, yes. Yes, I would! I would be happy to sell one of our islands."

"The island I'm thinking of caught my eye because it took us a long time to pass as we came around the channel into Nuku'alofa," I said.

"I know which one you mean," he replied.

"How much would that island be? How much would you sell me that for?"

"My friend," he said. "I would not sell you that island for any amount of money, because no one, no matter how rich they are, could afford to live there."

"Do you mind me asking why?" I said.

"You see, it is a one-volcano peak island." He explained: on one-volcano peak islands, all the rainwater washes off the sides of the mountain and back into the sea. There's no natural way to collect it, so the island is uninhabitable. Water is too heavy and expensive to transport it by human means. On two-volcano peak islands, though, a pool or a lake always forms in the valley between the two peaks, where it's possible to collect fresh water and build a house or even a village.

He added, "You pick out some other island, and I will tell you. I will tell you the price."

"That's great, I appreciate it. Let's say I find one as the ship is leaving and I come back to you. How much would you sell an otherwise uninhabited, two-volcano island somewhere close to Nuku'alofa so I could be around you and your people?"

"Oh, something close to Nuku'alofa would be $100,000 U.S." he boomed.

"Great. King, I will be back with you on this. I am most interested!"

The king let out another laugh, and to my surprise, asked me if I'd join him in getting a drink at the bar. I agreed. I'll be darned if we didn't soon find ourselves standing there in the ballroom over cocktails, chatting and laughing like we were old friends. He treated everyone with such kindness and respect. What a scene that must have been for the other passengers: to see the stowaway rubbing elbows with royalty! That was one of the greatest moments of my life. At that time, the whole world felt like it stretched before me. I didn't realize that it wouldn't extend past the island chain of Fiji, which was our next stop, and the scene of my final, fateful confrontation with Captain Blight.

The person who might have been most amused by my interaction with the King of Tonga was the Commodore of the P&O fleet. As the cruise company's highest ranking official on the ship, he was the master of ceremonies for the royal reception and stood near the king most of the time. The commodore and I became quite friendly, given our mutual friendship with Seamus, and I was incredibly thankful to him for pulling the strings to grant me a stateroom on the posh B deck. So, when the event finally came to an end, the two of us began getting to know each other, and we left the ballroom as drunken best friends, arm-in-arm.

As we walked down the hallway past the exit, we passed none other than Captain Blight himself. He was completely shocked at the sight before his eye—of me, buddying up to his boss. Blight's upright, military stride broke ever so slightly, for just a second, and his shoulders slumped, before he caught himself and regained his posture and composure. He shot me a laser beam of a look, then continued his brisk walk as if he had never crossed our paths.

For all I know, Captain Blight was a good man. Maybe he volunteered at orphanages whenever he got home. Maybe he knitted scarves for the elderly in his free time. Maybe he had a family, somewhere, who he loved dearly. I held no grudge against him, nor do I now. Yet he hated me with the red-eyed fury of an angry bull. And he was determined to find a way, somehow, to get me off that ship—even if it meant making every single passenger and crew member, as well as his boss, the commodore, hating him for it.

Not that I dwelled on that momentary exchange for very long. I was living large in the South Pacific and making new friends and seeing new places. The ship's next stop was Fiji, about a thousand miles north of New Zealand.

What a stupendous place! The country consists of more than 300 palm-shaded islands, about 100 of which are inhabited (meaning they must have at least two volcanoes, I guess), covering an area of ocean larger than California.

Fiji was first settled by Polynesians a few thousand years ago, probably before they moved on to Tonga and Hawaii—following the currents and the opposite path of my migration. It became a British colony in the 19th century until gaining its independence in 1970. Though known centuries ago as a place where cannibalism was regularly practiced, its people today are as warm as the tropical breezes that envelope their wonderful islands.

# CHAPTER XVII

# Nauseatingly American

*"You know you are truly alive when
you're living among lions."*

—Karen Blixen

**AFTER ANOTHER LONG** voyage at sea, the Canberra docked in the morning beside the country's surprisingly cosmopolitan capital of Suva, on the mountainous island of Viti Levu. As soon as the ship was tied to the docking pier, the crew put the ramps down and extended the gangways to allow the passengers to disembark. I wasn't allowed to leave the ship, of course, so I cheerily stayed in my stateroom and caught extra sleep as crowds of people made their way onto the dry land of Fiji.

Unbeknownst to me, one of those who disembarked was the ship's first mate. Earlier that day, Captain Blight had pulled him aside and said something to the effect of, "if you ever want to be promoted, if you ever want a raise, if you ever want to keep your job, then you're going to go to the American Consulate as soon as we land and make the U.S. government take responsibility for Mr. Van Cleve. I don't care what you say or what you have to do; see that it happens, or don't come back to the ship."

The first officer, preferring to keep his job, did as he was told and walked straight to the consulate after getting off the ship. The consul at that time was an outgoing, funny, and wonderfully likable African-American man in his early forties, from Philadelphia. A job like his, on the edge of paradise, is only given to people with high-level political connections because it's so cushy. After all, what kinds of diplomatic troubles could ever happen between Fiji and the U.S.? This consul relished his position.

From the moment he first landed in Fiji until that morning, the consul had never performed an official act on behalf of the American government. He had earned his government paycheck simply by being the face of the U.S., running the consulate. In turn, he enjoyed the life of being one of the country's top five percent income earners. He kept a beautiful hilltop mansion with massive, picturesque windows that looked onto an expansive, green farm valley. It was a party palace, and beautiful island women rolled in and out of the place all the time like it was the Playboy Mansion. In the swinging mid-1970s, in the age of disco, free love, bell bottoms, and good times, the consul was as cool as cool could be.

Most of the time, he never bothered going to the office. There was no need because nothing ever happened on Fiji. Still, when the first officer arrived at the consulate that morning, only the consul's secretary was there.

"I'm here to see the consul," the first officer told her. "I'm with the SS Canberra, and my captain told me only to address him."

"Well, he's not here right now," she replied.

"When would he be back? I'll wait."

"Well, he doesn't come in that often . . . "

"You need to call him, then," the first officer said, seeing his career flash before his eyes.

"He's not reachable by phone all the time," she said.

"Make. An. Effort." said the first officer, sternly.

"I can't reach him by phone," the secretary insisted.

"Then how do you get in contact with him?"

"Usually I just talk to him when he comes in."

"Then when is he due to come in?"

"Well, I'm not really certain."

The conversation, from what I was later told, was like an Abbott and Costello routine. Eventually the frustrated first mate simply said, "Fine then, I'll sit here and wait until the consul arrives." And he did just that, plopping himself onto a chair in the consulate's waiting room until the office closed at 5:00 p.m.

As the secretary prepared to leave, he asked her if she had heard from the consul yet. Her answer was an embarrassed, but clear, "No." No. The first officer knew that he couldn't go back to the ship empty-handed or else he'd be looking for a new line of work. His only option was to find another way to make contact with the consul outside of business hours. With nowhere else to turn, he crossed the street to a bar opposite the consulate and proceeded to get drunk. Between rounds of drinks, he started asking for people who might know the consul and where to track him down.

Another drinker piped up, "I know him. He's a great guy. He lives over in the hills in such-and-such neighborhood, and everybody loves him. We don't see him around here much, but every once in a while, he'll come in for a cocktail."

The first mate stowed the information in his drink clouded head, before spending a very enjoyable night on the island. At 9:00 a.m. the next day, he showed up again at the consulate, right when the doors opened, and approached the secretary.

"Were you able to reach the consul?" he asked.

"No," she said.

"Well, then I'm going to find him. Can you tell me precisely where he lives? I know which neighborhood but not the exact location."

"I can't help you. You do whatever you think you need to do but I am not allowed to give you that kind of information."

"I understand," he said, and left the building.

From the curb, he hailed a cab and took it into the hills where the American consul was reported to live. After some searching, and getting directions from the locals, he finally struck upon the correct house, which was located up a high-incline dirt road. The first mate knocked on the door, but there was no answer. At that exact moment, unbeknownst to the first mate, two women were joining the consul in his bed, and he wasn't going to be interrupted under any circumstances. The first mate knocked again. Still no answer. Then the first mate pounded at the door. Silence. The first mate pounded louder, like a sledgehammer banging into the thick, ornately carved mahogany.

A male voice rose from inside the house, "Whoever's at the front door, go the fuck away!"

One of the girls climbed off the bed, put on a silky robe, and opened the door to see where 'the fire' was. She saw only the first officer, in his dress whites, standing in front of her, with a polite British smile on his face. "I'm here to see the American consul," he said.

"He's not here," the girl replied.

"Well, then, I'm going to wait, and I'm going to wait inside, and there's nothing you can do to stop me," the first mate said, and he barged through the door.

The consul had no choice but to respond at this point, so he slipped on some shorts and walked into the front foyer. Angry from being pulled away from his three-person party, he demanded to know what was going on. The first officer carefully explained his situation with the captain, and finished by saying, "This is an urgent matter of state, and it requires your immediate attention."

The consul replied, "Well, you're in Fiji, and if it's urgent to you, it sure as hell doesn't mean that it's urgent to me. Let me take a shower and get dressed, then we'll see what this is all about." The first mate waited on the living room couch and a short while later, the consul appeared in presentable dress, then said goodbye to his female companions, and took a ride to the gleaming SS Canberra, docked in the harbor, where I was still unaware of the events taking place.

The first mate led the consul onto the ship and through the maze of halls and stairwells that led into the captain's office. Blight had been waiting for them, his blood pressure rose with every passing minute. Hardly before the consul could even take his seat upon entering the room, the captain unleashed his fury, ranting about the stowaway on board, who, "we have reason to believe is an American."

"What do you mean you've got reason to believe he's American?" the consul asked.

"Because I have seen his driver's license. He's twenty-one years old, and he came aboard my ship in Hawaii."

"Where's his passport, then?" Ah yes, the million-dollar question! I still can't hear the query without thinking about that moment.

"There is none, but he is an American citizen. He is your responsibility."

"No, he's not my responsibility. You have reason to believe he's an American, but I may not share that opinion." The consul had one of the cushiest U.S. government jobs ever created. He had no desire to get entangled in some international incident involving a British cruise ship docked at a Fiji port. He tried to wash his hands of the situation, but Blight refused to let him.

"You talk to him. You'll see. He's very American. *Nauseatingly American.*"

Tired of being screamed at, the consul finally agreed to see me. I was beckoned from my stateroom and led to the ship's best nightclub, where he waited for me. There was no way the captain, who couldn't stand the sight of me, was going to hold this meeting in his office. The consul and I shook hands. The whole scene seemed so surreal.

There I was, meeting with a high-ranking U.S. State Department official in an empty room decorated with a disco ball, mirrored walls, velvet sofas, and a long wooden dance floor on the coast of Fiji. We had a pleasant conversation, and the consul was genuinely amused by the situation. It certainly added some spice to his everyday routine, but he openly admitted that he didn't know what, in his official capacity as a representative of the American government, to do.

I explained that the ship had called ahead to every

port, and they all refused to take me. If he simply did nothing, and refused to accept responsibility, I'd have a free cruise to Southampton, England. "I've got the perfect life on this ship," I said. "I've got friends, lovers, and neighbors. I'm making money through just having conversations with people. I'm in freakin' heaven. Please, please, leave this alone."

He gladly agreed to steer clear and not take responsibility. "God bless you! God bless you!" I said. "When this is all over, I'm going to come back here, and we're going out to have a big time together."

With business settled, the two of us swapped stories about our adventures that had led both of us to that very moment in time, sitting together in the disco of the SS Canberra, docked in the harbor of the largest town, on a truly magical South Pacific Island. I described how I was just a Virginia boy who decided to travel west. I told him about Harry's, how I first spotted the ship in Hawaii and the way I snuck aboard. He recounted his two years as consul, and his near-perfect life, which included the two beautiful Fijian women who were in his bed when the first mate knocked on his door.

When we finished our highly entertaining conversation, he walked into the captain's office and told Blight, "I'm not interested in your problem." The consul then turned his back on the raging, screaming, red-faced captain, left the room, marched down the Canberra's gangplank, and got off the ship.

Blight, of course, didn't think the matter was over. Not by a long shot. In protest, he told the crew, "Until Guy Van Cleve leaves this ship, it is not moving." He was planting his feet in Suva, even if it meant causing an international incident. The Canberra was scheduled to set sail that evening, but it didn't. To the surprise of everyone on board—and to the port authorities and local officials as well—it stayed tied to the dock.

Meanwhile, Blight was maniacally working the phones to force a solution that would meet with his approval— an end with me removed from the Canberra. He called the U.S. State Department in Washington, DC, but no one there was interested in talking to a raving British lunatic. He then called a connection with the UK Foreign Secretary's Home Office, who in turn, had a connection, who in turn, had a connection, and so on. Eventually the proper channels were used to link British diplomats with the U.S. State Department and finally the phone rang at the Fiji Consulate. The consul's secretary was able to reach him for this one.

Late the following day, the consul returned to the ship and met with me again in the nightclub. "Look, I got a call from Washington," he said. "The captain has raised all sorts of hell through London, and the Brits contacted my boss. He told me that I've got to do something here. Action must be taken. I hate to tell you this, but . . . "

"No!" I interrupted. "Please! You don't understand!"

He wouldn't listen. "At the end of the day, I've got this fabulous gig here, and I'm not going to jeopardize it for you. If our roles were reversed, I know you'd be doing the same thing. I hate like hell to do it. I don't want to do it. I don't even know what the hell do to with you once I take you off the ship, but I'm probably going to have to take you off the ship."

"I'll live with the 'probably' part," I said. "Just please, do what you can."

I retired to my stateroom, sadder than a cowboy with an empty canteen in the middle of the desert and tried to catch a nap. A couple of hours later, I heard a knock on the door. I was instructed to leave the ship at 8:00 a.m. the next morning.

# CHAPTER XVIII

# Secrets in a Suitcase

*"Life shrinks or expands in proportion to one's courage."*

—Anais Nin

**IT DIDN'T TAKE** long for word to spread throughout the SS Canberra of my departure the next morning. I didn't doubt the consul's empathy for me, but there was no way he was going to put his job on the line to extend some twenty-one-year-old's stowaway adventure on a cruise ship. My first emotion upon hearing the news was complete and utter sadness. I decided to walk off the blues a little and savor my last few hours as a passenger by walking the decks above my stateroom. While there, I ran into one of my friends among the crew.

"Everybody's talking about this being your last night. We're going to throw you a going-away party like you've never seen before," he said.

"Sure, that's fine," I said, glumly. But even the prospect of a big bash in my honor could barely cheer me up.

"Come on down to the crew's mess at 7:30. We have

a dinner planned. Then we'll go straight to the Pigsty," he told me.

I have to admit, the prospect of letting off some steam there, among friends with a party in my honor, did seem inviting.

At the arranged time, around 7:30 p.m., I descended to the crew's mess and was welcomed like a long-lost friend by about fifty or sixty off-duty crew members. Hugs and handshakes were shared all around, along with more than a few off-color comments about Captain Blight. Resting upon the picnic tables was a veritable food orgy that had been prepared. If heaven has a smell, it would be exactly like the aromas wafting through that room on that evening; I was touched. Being a polite Southern boy, and not wanting to offend, I ate. And ate. And ate. I must have polished off five lobsters, and nearly as much cracked crab.

And all of that eating made me thirsty, of course, so, I drank. And drank. And drank. Somewhere between my first and seventh beer, my mood perked up a bit. By the time the meal been finished, the entire group navigated its way to the Pigsty, and I was feeling no pain. Most of the other partygoers were in a similar state, and we really cut loose. The Rolling Stones and other British Invasion music blared from six-foot-tall speakers hung in the corners, and colored lights flashed. People danced both on the large dancefloor and atop the wooden tables.

The rallying cry among the crew that night was, "Fuck the Captain!"

I can't say that I completely disagreed with the sentiment, but a part of me had already moved on. If I had learned nothing else in my life to this point, it was that as soon as the door to one adventure closes, another one opens. I made the best of that moment amongst my friends, in a corner of the world I had previously only dreamt of seeing, for as long as possible, relishing every last person and interaction. As more and more crew members ended their shift for the evening, they joined the festivities so that by midnight, you couldn't take two steps without bumping into someone. Nobody cared. The place felt like Times Square on New Year's Eve.

Around midnight, the party paused as the crew presented me with an engraved plaque to commemorate my voyage. This was just a brief intermission. One o'clock rolled around, and the party didn't slow. Two o'clock, and it was still going. Three o'clock came, and everyone was shit-faced and full of energy. Shortly after this, with only four-plus hours before my departure, two male crew members stood on a table and turned down the blaring music to make an announcement. They held a mysterious object behind them. One of the men was a short, powerful guy who I was friendly with, but I didn't know too well. The other was my good friend, the Jamaican named Peter. He stood about my height, around six feet, and was the radio man who originally called ahead to all the ports to find out if any country would take responsibility for me. Peter was one of my very closest friends on the ship and let me borrow jeans and shirts as we were identical sizes.

"Hey Guy, we want you to know that you're a hero in our eyes," Peter said, then gave a fun, rambling speech fueled by alcohol and true affection.

Afterward, the other guy chimed in, "We want to give you a going-away present, so you'll remember us and this crew forever!" They revealed the mysterious object they had been holding: it was the ship's flag. In the dark of night, the two of them had apparently shimmied up the cruise ship's flagpole and secured it for me as a present. When the rest of the crew saw what Peter and the other guy held in their hands, they erupted in laughter and cheer—as if England's soccer team had just won the World Cup.

The gift was a tremendous act of rebellion against the captain. A ship's flag is the highest flag a vessel flies when it's at sea. When it comes into port, the ship is not allowed to dock or anchor unless the flag is clearly showing in order to identify itself. To this day, the invaluable, gifted flag has been hanging on a wall in my home, framed in glass, ever since.

The music blared, and the crowd bobbed and danced for another hour before finally beginning to lose steam. As the crowd dissolved, Seamus approached and nodded toward the flag and gift plaque I had cradled beneath my arm.

"How are you going to take those things with you off the ship?" he asked into my ringing ear.

"I don't know. I didn't even think about it," I said.

Seamus then announced to the straggling partygoers, "Guy needs a suitcase!" The irony was too perfect . . . I had snuck on board without a suitcase, which Captain Blight refused to believe, and now they were going to make sure that I left *with* one (not that I even realized the irony at that time). Word spread faster than Newton's apple hitting the ground. "Guy needs a suitcase! Guy needs a suitcase!"

In short order, Peter presented me with a weathered piece of light blue luggage covered in stickers from destinations from around the world: Johannesburg, Indonesia, Hong Kong, the Philippines, Madagascar. By this time, the sun's rays were already creeping above the horizon. Dawn would soon be upon us soon. Most of my friends wished me farewell so they could catch a couple of hours of sleep before their next shift, and the last of them half-guided, half-carried me back to my stateroom. Before collapsing on my bed with full onset exhaustion, I drunkenly shoved my few articles of clothing and my new presents into the suitcase and snapped it shut. That was all I needed to pack.

Around 7:30 a.m., I was jolted out of my sleep by violent banging at my door. Weak-kneed and still tipsy, I staggered across the stateroom, turned the doorknob, and opened it to see my two stern-faced escorts—though they were without their sidearms.

"We're here to take you to the captain's office."

"Okay. I understand," I slurred.

I turned to grab my suitcase, and we left. I must have been quite a sight walking through the ship's hallways. My clothes were booze-soaked and wrinkled from the wild night before, and because I had passed out (not really slept) in them. My eyes were bloodshot and puffy, and my hair was not well combed. On top of all that, the smell of alcohol oozed from every pore of my body.

The American consul was seated in the reception area when I arrived at my destination, while the secretary was stationed behind her desk.

"Well, look at what the cat dragged in," he said with a smile.

"Yeah, there was a going-away party," I said.

"You look three sheets to the wind!"

"I know, and I feel that way."

At precisely 8:00 a.m., the intercom on the secretary's desk buzzed, and the captain's voice blasted from its speaker. "Send in the American consul."

The two of us eyed each other, then he stood up and entered the captain's office. I could see the whole scene through the doorway from my seat. Blight approached the consul with a set of papers in his hand and crisply said in a prim-and-proper tone, "Sir, I am Captain Blight of the SS Canberra, and I now officially turn to your charge an American citizen."

The consul signed the papers, accepting and acknowledging the transfer of one crazy son-of-a-bitch named Guy Van Cleve. The captain graciously waved for him to have a seat, then barked to the secretary, "Have Mr. Van Cleve come in."

That was the first time he had ever used my name, even though the words were dripping with contempt. To that point, I was always, "Sir." As in, "Sir! What are you doing here?" "Sir! What makes you think you can stow away on my ship?"

"Sir! Where is your passport?" "Sir! Where is your luggage?"

The man despised me. On more than one occasion, crew members heard him say that if so many people hadn't known of my existence, he would have thrown me overboard without a second thought– and he was serious. He would've happily made me vanish if he had been able.

I stumbled into Blight's office and took a seat next to the American consul. The captain kept his good eye on his desk during my entrance, not once acknowledging my presence. Sitting next to me was my suitcase. I didn't think to leave it in the reception area. Finally, the captain raised his head, but before his gaze met me, it caught the suitcase. This was when I realized the irony of it.

Blight, of course, thought that the suitcase had to be the missing luggage he was searching for all along. The missing luggage that probably cost him untold tens of thousands of dollars in overtime pay, as he forced the crew to ransack the entire ship. The missing luggage that held my passport. His face turned red, and he began to steam like a teakettle. Blight kept staring at that suitcase, his body as still as a statue. Seconds passed. A minute. The consul and I watched him in silence. Finally, after about 90 seconds, he looked at me, gritting his teeth and shaking his head.

I tried to climb out of my fog to string some words of explanation together.

"Captain, this isn't my suitcase!" I finally said. "I just picked up some souvenirs and clothes along the way that the crew gave me. The suitcase was a gift!" The captain kept mildly shaking and turning his head with slight angles of intensified glares, and he stared daggers at my suitcase, then at me, then my suitcase, and so on.

"This suitcase has stickers from around the world on it," I continued. "I haven't been all around the world. I'm from Virginia, and I went to Hawaii and I met you. I haven't been to these places. It's not my suitcase."

He still wasn't buying what I was selling. "Go ahead, you can look inside it!" I stated. Being so drunk, I had forgotten that the ship's flag was inside of it. The gravity of my offer was lost on me; if the captain *had* opened the suitcase and discovered the ship's flag, I would not be alive right now. There is no doubt in my mind that he would have strangled me by my neck until dead, witnesses and consequences be damned.

Blight ignored my words, thank goodness, and turned to the Consul, "I now hand responsibility of Mr. Van Cleve to the United States Government," he said through gritted teeth. "Good day. You two are dismissed."

# CHAPTER XIX

# Chickens and Pigs on a Plane

*"The biggest adventure you can take is
to live the life of your dreams."*

—Oprah Winfrey

**THE DOORS TO** the office swung open, and the consul and I rose from our seats and walked out. We were escorted through the ship by the two guards, while I shook hands with crew members in the hallways as we passed along the way.

We reached the gangplank, which dropped at a nearly forty-five-degree angle onto the old, low-lying concrete wharf and looked as steep as a ski slope to an inebriated soul like myself. I carefully began to walk down it, hands gripped to the railings, when I heard a commotion from the decks above. Hundreds of passengers had risen from bed early and gathered to wish me well. They yelled, "So long, Guy," and "Bon Voyage!" They even threw streamers passed out to them by the crew. I felt like a departing rock star.

At the base of the gangplank sat a taxicab, waiting to take us to the consulate. We reached it, and the consul and I turned to awe at the glimpse of the massive crowds on the rails of the promenade deck and the two decks above it overlooking the harbor. A look of astonishment was painted on both our faces.

"This is all for you?" he questioned.

"These are the people I met and the friends I made. Can you believe it?"

"No, I can't. This is way cool," he said. Coming from him, that was quite a compliment.

I gave the crowd one final, heartfelt wave goodbye as the two of us climbed into the cab and drove off. I've never had a more impactful moment in my life than seeing the outpouring of affection from those passengers and crew—people whose lives I had clearly touched, and whose lives profoundly touched mine, in such a short amount of time.

The cab wound its way through the narrow streets of Suva. I was on land again, but I could still feel the ship's gentle rocking beneath me. I looked out the window at the apartment buildings and retail shops and restaurants, where the day's activity were just beginning. I turned to the consul. "Okay, what now?" I asked.

"I really don't know," he replied.

The consul and I went directly to the consulate, but we didn't stay there very long. I sat in the lobby area while he disappeared into his office, where he must have plotted out a plan for me. He emerged a short while later with a green piece of paper in his hand, carrying the official seal of the U.S. consul for Fiji. He handed it to me.

"This is the first time I've ever used my official seal. Maybe it'll help you," he said.

I looked at the paper. On it, his secretary had typed two short sentences: "Please allow Mr. Van Cleve back into the USA. We have reason to believe he is an American citizen." That was it. *We have reason to believe he is an American citizen.* This was to be my passport. "I can't say if this will get you back into the country, but with your people skills, it should. I'm not worried," the consul told me.

"Great," I said, folding the paper and slipping it into the back pocket of my blue jeans, still a little unsure as to why I'd need it or how I'd use it, having never gone through customs or immigration before.

"The American government is going to fly you home," he explained.

I would be flying from the airstrip in Suva to Nadi, which was the international airport on the western end of the island. From there, I was to take a jet back to Hawaii. Traveling further west would have to wait.

We left the consulate and rode this time in the back of a dark, American-made sedan –probably the consul's official government car– to the tiny Suva airport. The route took us through the glory of Fiji, all palm tree forests, and large, open fields draped by jade green mountains backed by heavenly blue skies. The two of us talked in the back seat, and he apologized for forcing me from the ship.

"I understand," I assured him. "It's okay."

The car finally made a sharp turn onto a bumpy dirt road, and the Suva airport appeared before us. Except it was more of a giant, open field than an airport. The terminal was a bus stop bench with an overhang above it to protect up to three people from the rain. The car stopped at the edge of the field, and we exited the car. I didn't see a single sign of life.

"This is the airfield," the consul said.

"You're kidding, right?"

"No, this is the Suva airport. The plane will be here in about a half-hour. Just to prepare you, it's kind of an unorthodox flight."

"In what way?"

"The plane doesn't really have any seats . . . it's more of a cargo plane, but there will be lots of passengers–and more."

"What do you mean 'and more?'" I said.

He smiled. "You'll see. I'll see, too. I'm going with you to Nadi."

I told him it wasn't necessary, but he insisted that it was. Once I had been placed in his custody, he had a responsibility to make sure that I got on the plane—and didn't get hassled for not having a passport. Regardless, we had a fine time shooting the breeze beneath the tropical South Pacific sun on a magnificent, memorable morning. The minutes passed, and the other passengers started arriving. Then more. Many of them had brought livestock—like pigs and chickens—along for the ride. I couldn't believe what I was seeing.

At the appropriate time, a silver, two-propeller Air Pacific plane dropped from the sky and bounced-landed on the dusty strip of dirt and grass designated as the runway. It came to a complete stop, then a cargo door dropped from the back for the unloading and loading of passengers and cargo. The consul and I quickly scurried on board, and the inside was exactly as he described it—empty of seats and completely open. Sitting on the left and right wheel hubs was considered "first class seating." Once the other passengers finished climbing inside with their cargo, the pilot closed the door, and then they let their animals loose, free range, inside the plane. Chickens were flying around everywhere, and pigs chasing them.

The flight lasted only a half-hour or so, then we landed at Nadi, a real airport. The consul and I let the others disembark first, then we walked to the terminal and found a table at a restaurant. We had several hours to kill before my flight to Hawaii, and I had money to burn. I had left the ship with more than £1,500 worth of British pound notes, generously given to me by the passengers during my stay. Needless to say, the consul and I enjoyed a very nice, leisurely lunch. At the end, I picked up the tab and tried to leave a nice tip. I soon learned that tipping was taboo in Fiji. It was a long-standing, cultural ethic which honored the belief that good service was to be expected, rather than rewarded.

When the airline began boarding the Hawaii flight, the consul walked me all the way to my seat, identifying himself to the gate agents and telling them he was there on official business. I didn't have any problems with identification or a passport, thanks to him. With that, his work was done. The consul gave me a hearty embrace and shook my hand.

"Good luck! Have more great adventures!" he said.

"I will. I promise," I replied.

Of the roughly 500 seats that occupy a typical Boeing 747, only about fifty passengers filled this one, meaning there was plenty of room to stretch out. Once the nine-hour flight to Hawaii took off, I asked the young flight attendant if I could raise the armrests in my back row seat so I could lie down. She winked, smiled, and said it would be fine, so I did, and finally caught up on much-needed sleep. I don't even remember takeoff.

I must have been out for a couple of hours before I finally opened my eyes again; we were soaring at 30,000 feet above the Pacific. Feeling more refreshed and friendly, I began talking to the flight attendant.

"You serve Bloody Mary's on this flight?" I asked.

"Yeah. Of course," she said.

She returned a couple of minutes later with a drink in-hand. She placed it on my tray table and plopped onto the seat next to mine. "I've just got to ask: why was an American official escorting you onto the plane?"

She was quite attractive, I must say—brown hair with a fit body, accentuated by the form-fitting stewardess outfit of the time—and, given that there were almost no passengers in sight of her section, she was bored. I told her the cliff notes of my entire story. What a hell of an icebreaker that was for me! As we got to talking, a sort of spark had ignited between us. She kept the drinks flowing, and before I knew it, we were fooling around on the plane. Once again, another door of opportunity opened just as the one behind me closed.

The plane landed in Honolulu late in the afternoon, and my heart pounded as I walked through the terminal towards immigration and customs. I was more than a little uncertain about how I would get past the officers with no passport and just a green piece of paper signed by the consul. Not knowing my way around the airport, I intentionally became the last passenger from the plane to get in the line at immigration so I could observe all the happenings. When it was time to step up to the booth, I realized all of my concerns were unfounded, and I breezed right past the agent—a tanned, beautiful young Hawaiian woman.

She didn't even look at the consul's note, but she did

look at me with a beautiful smile. As I was last in line, we chatted about me riding my motorcycle all over Oahu's mountainous land and seascapes, and I asked if she would be up to do that one day with me on her day off. She said yes and gave me her phone number. "Give me a call sometime," she said, smiling mischievously as I exited. The whole scene was amazingly informal. At the curb outside the terminal, I hailed a cab and took it to Harry's, where I expected my motorcycle to still be chained to the set of pipes outside the back of the bordello. I was wrong. The bike was gone.

Not knowing what to do, or where to go next, I entered the building and walked up the steps to the bordello. When Harry first laid eyes upon me, he looked at me like he saw a ghost.

"You're alive! You're alive!" he yelled, hugging me so tightly that I got a mouthful of polyester from his flowery Hawaiian shirt. "Jay said you were dead. He said you were long dead!"

"Well, as you can see, I'm not dead!"

"Is any of my stuff still here? And where's my motorcycle?"

Harry told me that Jay got a pair of bolt cutters and had made off with my bike. He and Glenn hadn't been seen in the neighborhood in a long time. I was dumbstruck. I had promised Jay he could keep the motorcycle only if he lit himself on fire and created a diversion to help get me onto the ship. There was no fire, and no diversion, and I jumped on the Canberra without any help from him. He stole my bike! *That scoundrel.*

Harry, under the impression I was dead, had cleaned out all the clothes and belongings that I had stored at the bordello. I had nothing but the contents of my suitcase.

Exhausted and out of options, I went to the YMCA and rented a room so I could collapse and fall asleep. Over the next couple of days, a bunch of the regular residents at the Y, who I knew from earlier, filled in some of the details on Glenn and Jay. Both had left the island shortly after I departed on the Canberra and went back to Glenn's home state of Washington. They took my bike with them.

One of the Y regulars, a guy everyone called the "Crazy Indian," told me to find out if I had insurance on it. *Insurance.* I hadn't even thought of that. I called the Yamaha dealer, and they confirmed that I had, in fact, bought insurance, as required by Hawaiian law for any registered motor vehicle to get a license tag. The cost was included in the original purchase price. I went back and told the Crazy Indian.

He said, "Your bike was stolen. Everybody knows it's in Washington State. If you really want it back, report it to the FBI. It's an interstate thing. Worst case, you'll get the insurance money for it."

Following his advice, I went to the local FBI office in downtown Honolulu and reported the interstate theft of a vehicle. The agent thought I was full of shit at first because apparently nobody had apparently ever stolen a motorcycle off the island before. After convincing him that I was being honest, he filled out a report. Then I filled out a claim with State Farm, which was the company that insured my bike. As fate would have it, the Yamaha dealer had sold me a premium policy, and upon investigating my claim, State Farm refunded me for my bike in full—every nickel and penny, down to the sales tax and cost of the license plate—all in one fat check. *But what to do with the money?* I considered continuing west and buying a ticket to Australia. I found out, though, that non-citizens can't purchase a one-way flight to the country because the government doesn't want people to linger (or malinger) there forever. For that reason, I would also be required to buy a return ticket. Even with the insurance payout, I didn't have enough money to comfortably cover the cost of a roundtrip flight to Australia *and* stay there very long.

Then, another idea struck me: the check was big enough to easily buy me a ticket to California, a place that I had never explored. From the lobby of the YMCA, I called Steve Sweat, one of my buddies from Lynchburg who was now a student at the University of California in Northridge. To my relief, he answered.

We caught up briefly, and then I said, "I've done Honolulu, and I'm thinking about going to Los Angeles next."

He instantaneously offered me a place to stay, and that was the key I needed to my next adventure.

Perfect! I went to the airport with my suitcase, filled with little more than the flag, the plaque the crew gave me, and a couple of shirts and jeans. I bought a ticket to Southern California and was about to live out a Jim Morrison-sized dream in LA. Now, at that time in history, that was one fabulous open *Door* worth walking through.

I discovered, once again, that if you walk down the road of colors and textures, life has a way of meeting you in that lushness. Whether you're hopping on the top of a boxcar, jumping aboard the world's largest luxury cruise liner, or whimsically taking a flight to the City of Angels, life can be summed up by my motto, SHAWOWO (shit has a way of working out).

shawowo

CANBERRA
P&O
LINES
1975
LONDON

# ABOUT THE AUTHOR

Since exploring distant and some forbidden places and as a child growing up in Lynchburg, Virginia, Guy Van Cleve has led a life governed by senses, daydreams, and boundless curiosities. Though his thirst for adventure may never subside, he is still fulfilling his life's mission, day by day, to help inspire others to enjoy—and *live*—life to the fullest. *Roam Wasn't Built in a Day* is the first in a series from his ever continuing true-life tales. Guy Van Cleve calls Atlanta home regardless of where he may next be found.